A NATURALIST'S GUIDE TO THE

BIRDS
OF
NEW ZEALAND

Oscar Thomas

JOHN BEAUFOY PUBLISHING

Photo credits
Front cover: *main image* Fiordland Crested Penguin; *bottom left* Northern Royal Albatross; *bottom centre* Takahe;
bottom right Shining Cuckoo. All © Oscar Thomas.
Title page: Whio © Oscar Thomas; **Contents page:** Kererū © Oscar Thomas; **Back cover:** Buller's Albatross ©
Oscar Thomas.

Photos are denoted by a page number followed by t (top), c (centre), b (bottom), l (left) or r
(right). All photos are by Oscar Thomas except:
Charlie Barnett 51tl, 66t, 74t, 80b, 84t, 136b. **Phil Battley** 52t, 107b. **Nick Beckwith** 20b, 37br, 75b, 115t,
137c. **Leon Berard** 13t, 14b, 22br. **David Boyle** 51tr, 81t, 82b, 83t, 89t, 93c, 93b, 98bl, 110tl, 136t, 137t. **Scott
Brooks** 29b, 64b, 73t, 89bl, 89br, 90t, 90b, 101t, 102b, 107t, 109t, 110tr. **Adam Colley** 55b, 58b, 59b, 112br,
121br. **Max de Beer** 15t. **Igor Debski** 99b. **Matthias Dehling** 15b, 26br, 69bl. **George Hobson** 14t, 23c, 83b,
125l. **Qin Huang** 13b. **Giverny Kate Forbes** 98br, 116b, 117b. **Allan MacGillivray** 127b. **Darren Markin** 12b,
66bl, 67c, 149b. **Colin O'Donnell** 36b. **Bradley Shields** 13c, 16t, 21br, 22bl, 49tr, 50b, 53tl, 68tr, 71tl, 71tr,
71b, 131b, 140r. **Aaron Skelton** 60b, 109b. **David Thomas** 4b, 28t, 153t. **Imogen Warren** 19b, 27b, 44tr, 44b,
52c, 61t, 64t, 65bl, 65br, 69br, 119tl, 121bl, 122b, 123c, 124t.

ISBN 978-1-913679-41-5

Edited by Krystyna Mayer
Designed by Alpana Khare Graphic Design
Project management by Rosemary Wilkinson

Printed and bound in Malaysia by Times Offset (M) Sdn. Bhd.

·Contents·

INTRODUCTION

Aotearoa New Zealand is home to some of the most unique and fascinating avifauna on the planet. This stems from a combination of 80 million years of isolation (Australia, the nearest land mass, lies about 2,000km across the Tasman Sea), an increasingly varied climate ranging from subtropical to subantarctic, and a relatively recent history of human settlement.

During the Cretaceous Period, the immense supercontinent known as Gondwana split, and the (now primarily submerged) continent of Zealandia drifted far apart from the neighbouring realms of Australia and Antarctica, allowing the fauna, flora and geography of the land to evolve in isolation from the rest of the world.

Studies suggest that early Polynesians discovered Aotearoa in the years leading up to 1300AD, culminating a succession of exploratory voyages from the southern Pacific Islands. At this point, it was truly the land of the birds. The New Zealand wrens (Acanthisittidae) are thought to be some of the most ancient passerines, not to mention the bizarre ground-dwelling kiwi (Apterygidae), five species all flightless and nocturnal. Aside from birds, three tiny bat species were the only land mammals present, with seals, whales and dolphins abundant around the coast. Māori expansion led to the clearing of nearly 50 per cent of the native forest cover by fire on most of both main islands. Certain birds proved to be an easy food source, and nine moa species (Dinornithiformes), a gigantic, flightless, avian order, were quickly hunted to extinction. With them disappeared Haast's Eagle *Hieraaetus moorei*, the largest eagle ever to exist, which relied on moa to feed on.

When Captain James Cook arrived in the 1770s he noted that the bird song was deafening. The first European settlers also began to destroy precious habitats on a huge scale, until only 23 per cent of original forest cover remained. With them came terrestrial mammals such as rabbits, to hunt for their fur and meat. Their populations exploded, prompting a wave of predators to be brought from Europe to help control them, including stoats and weasels. Birds were discovered to be an easy source of food, and within a century the invasive predators plagued all corners of the country, causing many birds to be eradicated. Those that were not remain in serious trouble. New Zealand's avifauna was

kākāpō

poorly equipped to deal with such tampering with the ecosystem. Many of New Zealand's endemic birds evolved to become flightless or poor fliers, active during the night, and to be rather cryptic in appearance, as these traits were once favourable to survival. The kākāpō, for example, is unique in being the world's heaviest living parrot species, as well as the only one that is flightless, also being nocturnal, and exceedingly long lived. Its snap response to a potential predator is to freeze, relying on its impressive mottled green camouflage to conceal it on the forest floor. Although effective against vision-based avian predators that dominated New Zealand's skies before human arrival, this strategy does nothing to prevent an attack by mammalian predators that are alerted to prey by smell.

The environment is at the heart of New Zealand's identity, shaping its economy, lifestyles and culture. More and more visitors cite nature as a major reason for choosing the country as a holiday destination. Decline in biodiversity, however, has been rapid, leaving a legacy of love and loss. One third of New Zealand's endemic avifauna has become extinct since human arrival, the most damaging culprits being invasive animals, which kill an estimated 25 million native birds every year. The best efforts of legendary conservation pioneers could not save the Bush Wren and South Island Snipe, whose last island stronghold was invaded by ship rats in 1964. The added effects of fire, urbanization and overexploitation of resources have left a lasting impact.

Today, there is a major focus on ensuring that past mistakes are not repeated, and no more native species are lost. The government has developed a national Biodiversity Action Plan to help identify solutions aimed to halt and ultimately reverse the decline of indigenous fauna and flora. A range of methods is in play to reduce the impact that mammalian predators have on the country's wildlife. Traps and baits are the main techniques used, but in expansive areas and hard-to-access terrains, 1080 poison pellets are dropped aerially, targeting mammals and leaving no trace in the environment itself. Birds such as kiwi, North Island Kōkako and Yellowhead have benefited hugely from 1080 use.

Certain offshore and fenced mainland islands have shown significant success, with the complete eradication of mammalian predators within an area. Through the Department of Conservation (DOC), 8.6 million hectares of New Zealand have become designated public conservation land. Pest control in these zones laid the groundwork for the ambitious Predator Free 2050 project, with the end goal of eradicating invasive mammals from the country supported by both new and existing conservation efforts on a globally unprecedented scale. If the project were to be successful, it would reduce an economic drain of nearly NZ$3.3 billion annually, and leave an impressive conservation legacy for future generations.

SPECIES DESCRIPTIONS

Each species covered in this book is headed under a common name by which it is predominantly known in New Zealand (an alternative is listed for species recently renamed or known differently overseas), and a scientific (or binomial name). The first part of a scientific name is the genus, the second part refers to the species and the third, where applicable, refers to the subspecies (ssp.). Subspecific level has been included for birds that are resident, or certainly occur in New Zealand on a regular basis. A Māori name is given for birds where one is known. Their approximate length/height is given in centimetres.

The profiles provide a description of each bird, identifying features for males, females and immatures/juveniles, as well as distinguishing features for various subspecies, and breeding and non-breeding plumages in certain cases. Distribution across New Zealand is

Shore Plover, adult female

Shore Plover, adult male

detailed, and globally where applicable. There is information on how to locate the species by their preferred habitats for breeding, feeding and roosting, distinctive behaviour and diverse calls.

All entries contain the birds' conservation status in New Zealand, and note whether they are endemic, native, or introduced and naturalized. Endemic refers to the species that breed only in New Zealand, like the Shore Plover and Rifleman. Native birds are those that can also be found breeding elsewhere in the world, yet naturally occur in New Zealand, such as the White-fronted Tern, or are recent arrivals that have become established (self-introduced), such as the Welcome Swallow. Birds that are introduced and naturalized, like the Yellowhammer and Mallard, were brought to New Zealand through the aid of humans and have established in the wild. Exotic species were usually introduced by early European settlers for hunting, ornamental reasons or simply for nostalgia. Threats faced by endangered species are also described. This is not a definitive guide to the birds of New Zealand, but provides an introduction to 250 species, with emphasis placed on those that are unique, endemic, breeding locally and most regularly encountered in the field. A complete checklist of the birds of New Zealand (p. 161) lists close to 400 species that have been known to reach the country. In the descriptions, endemic species are indicated by a green symbol at the top of each bird entry.

Abbreviations used NI: North Island, NZ: New Zealand, SI: South Island; C: central, E: east, N: north, S: south, W: west, WS: wingspan.

GEOGRAPHY & CLIMATE

Aotearoa New Zealand is the sixth largest island nation on Earth, situated in the south-western Pacific Ocean. The two main islands are Te Ika-a-Māui/North Island and Te Waipounamu/South Island, separated by the Cook Strait. The third largest is Rakiura/Stewart Island, located 30km further south from what we will call 'the mainland' across Foveaux Strait. The numerous other islands are significantly smaller in area; however, the nation's combined land area comes to a total of 267,710km².

The approximately 600 islands that make up New Zealand all sit on an immense submerged portion of continental crust known as Te Riu-a-Māui/Zealandia, which itself resides on the boundary of the Pacific and Indo-Australian tectonic plates. New Zealand's modern land mass experienced severe uplift due to the constant unrest and grinding of the two plates (responsible for the phenomenon of earthquakes, which are not uncommon). This also displaced metamorphic rock along a 500km stretch of the South Island to create the Southern Alps. The highest peak is Aoraki/Mount Cook at 3,724m, not far from magnificent (yet shrinking) glaciers such as Franz Josef and Fox. Although the North Island is less mountainous, there is a sizable zone of geothermal activity in the centre featuring large caldera volcanoes such as huge Lake Taupo, which has a history of incredibly powerful eruptions.

Most of mainland New Zealand is encompassed by a temperate zone with four distinct seasons. Its location in a latitude zone with prevailing westerly winds, and tropical weather patterns, have a strong influence on the country's climate. This results in more variable weather patterns than in larger continental countries. Being surrounded by the Pacific Ocean, New Zealand has a maritime climate, with mild temperatures, moderate rainfall and plentiful sunshine. The mean average temperatures range from 10°C in the south to 16°C in the north, with an overall warming of 1.4°C recorded since 1909. The coldest month is usually July, the warmest January or February. There is relatively small variation between summer and winter temperatures, although for the semi-arid, more inland regions such as Central Otago there can be a variation of up to 14°C in one day, and an extreme low of -10°C. Temperatures also decrease by about 0.7°C for every 100m increase in altitude, with snowfall regular in subalpine and alpine regions during winter. Most areas of New Zealand have at least 2,000 hours of sunshine annually. Average rainfall is

Looking out over Whangapoua Beach from Mt Hobson, Aotea/Great Barrier Island

600–1,600mm, which is fairly evenly spread throughout the year. with a predominately dry period over the summer. In northern and central areas of New Zealand most of the rainfall occurs in winter, but the south experiences the least amount of rainfall during the winter season. The West Coast receives the strongest downpours, regularly exceeding 10,000mm near the mountains.

Habitats & Bird Communities

An impressive range of distinctive environments exists across New Zealand, catering to the diverse birdlife. Stretching from subtropical 29 degrees south to subantarctic 52 degrees south, the vast and prolific marine environment is unlike that of any other. Forty-three per cent of the world's seabird species breed in New Zealand territory, and many others use the waters as a migration pathway or to forage for food. While some species come close enough inshore to be seen from land, the best method for observing them is on a pelagic boat trip on the open ocean. Sightings depend strongly on timing and location, but the Antipodean Albatross, Yellow-eyed Penguin and New Zealand Storm Petrel are examples of some of the most sought after species.

Offshore and outlying islands can host an enormous variety of avifauna due to their isolation, with the subtropical broadleaved forests and exposed cliff tops of Rangitahua/Kermadec Islands to the north attracting birds like the Masked Booby and White-naped Petrel to breed. Rēkohu/Chatham Islands, 800km east of the mainland, is home to the Chatham Island Tāiko and Black Robin. The rare Shore Plover – once present all around New Zealand – became restricted to the Chatham Islands where it can be found on shore platforms and rocky coastlines. Rough farmland, expansive lagoons, peat bogs and dense forest are some examples of other environments found there. Five virtually pristine island

Rocky coast of Rangatira/South East Island, in the Chatham Islands

Mixed wader flock at Pūkorokoro Miranda
Wildlife Reserve

Winter scene at Mirror Lakes and Mt Eglinton,
Fiordland National Park

groups exist in the Southern Ocean, known as the New Zealand Subantarctic Islands: Tini Heke/Snares Islands, Moutere Māhue/Antipodes Islands, Moutere Hauriri/Bounty Islands, Maungahuka/Auckland Islands and Moutere Ihupuku/Campbell Islands. They offer bizarre twists on well-known birds, such as the Subantarctic Snipe and Reischek's Parakeet, inhabiting unique mega-herb fields and windswept tussock grassland, which also act as safe havens for numerous species of ocean-going seabirds during their breeding season.

Coastlines are of great importance as the meeting point of land and sea, and New Zealand holds the tenth longest of any nation. Migrating shorebirds such as Bar-tailed Godwits utilize the sheltered mudflats of estuaries and harbours at low tide to feed, retiring to roost on nearby exposed sandspits once the tide approaches. Banded Rails skulk through dense mangrove forests, and the ever-scarce Fairy Tern forages for fish in select river mouths and tidal inlets, brooding on sand dunes and shell banks with other species, including the Variable Oystercatcher. Rock stacks and cliffs provide safe nesting habitat for Red-billed Gulls and marine shags, and steep sounds bordered by boulder beaches in the south-west support populations of Fiordland Crested Penguins. Certain habitats have even been induced by birds, through seabird-burrowed soils and guano deposits. This phenomenon exists in dense seabird colonies such as those of Grey-faced Petrels in coastal forested headlands, and in the well-established colonies of Australasian Gannets.

Despite the loss of over 90 per cent of New Zealand's wetlands since human habitation, they remain some of the most diverse landscapes around. Well-vegetated freshwater lakes and river systems that span the country support Spotless Crakes and Australasian Bitterns, with New Zealand Scaup and grebe species seen more often out in open water. Braided riverbeds, a prominent feature of the South Island, are preferred breeding grounds for many species, including the Black-fronted Tern and Wrybill.

Upper Waimakariri River, Arthur's Pass

The enigmatic whio/Blue Duck lives in fast-flowing mountain rivers. Alpine species in the Southern Alps include the scree slope and rock garden-loving Rock Wren, and adaptive Kea, which move between mountain ridges, tussock grassland and native southern beech forests. The Brown Creeper and Yellow-crowned Parakeet also feed high in the canopy of such forests, while at night kiwi storm the undergrowth. At lower elevations the standard switches to podocarp forests, with a canopy dominated by emergent Rimu and Kauri trees in the north, the latter of which can grow to 55m tall. The Tomtit and North Island Kōkako favour this habitat.

Introduced species tend to favour modified environments that are close to what they might have lived in naturally overseas. Farmland and open country host Eurasian Skylarks and Australian Magpies, and huge numbers of native Swamp Harriers and endemic Paradise Shelducks, both of which have also profited from widespread forest clearance. Exotic pine plantations are supporting increasingly more pairs of New Zealand Falcons, while in urban areas and cityscapes the familiar Tūī thrive alongside Eurasian Blackbirds and Rock Pigeons.

Certain species, such as the New Zealand Pipit and Sacred Kingfisher, are connoisseurs of many different habitats, and others appear to be increasingly capable of adjusting to suit human-modified environments. It is difficult to travel anywhere in New Zealand and not see any birds at all. Once you gain confidence with identifying local birds, you can head further afield and discover all this beautiful country has to offer. For careful and detailed descriptions of specific locations to visit, be sure to refer to *The 50 Best Birdwatching Sites in New Zealand* by Liz Light and Oscar Thomas.

BIRD IDENTIFICATION

Many aspects should be taken into consideration when attempting to identify an unfamiliar species. Size, shape, colours, patterns, call, behaviour, habitat and location can all help an observation. Even taking note of the way birds walk or move in flight could be the clincher. The illustrations below show the most common ways to refer to certain parts of a bird to describe its physical appearance. Some species look very similar, like Cook's and Pycroft's Petrels, so always consider several options. A decent record photograph is useful for identification purposes, enabling you to share your sightings with others and receive a second opinion.

Topography of a Cook's Petrel (left) and New Zealand Pipit (right)

SUBMISSION OF RECORDS

www.birdsnz.org.nz/birding/rare-bird-sightings Birds New Zealand (Birds NZ) coordinates a rare bird reporting scheme on its website. If you happen across a wild bird that you cannot find in this book, or one far outside its normal range, submit an Unusual Bird Report (UBR) form online, or email your Regional Representative. The Records Appraisal Committee (RAC) will assess the sighting, and make a decision based on evidence presented. A searchable database of past records can be viewed at rare.birds.org.nz.

ebird.org/newzealand Run by the Cornell Lab of Ornithology, eBird is one of the world's largest biodiversity-related projects with more than 100 million records annually. Birders gather data on distribution, abundance, habitat and trends simply by uploading a checklist of all birds observed during an outing. Data quality is important, as these stats are used for scientific research, and the ambitious NZ Bird Atlas scheme.

North Island Brown Kiwi ■ *Apteryx mantelli* 40–65cm ⓔ
(kiwi-nui)

DESCRIPTION Rotund, ground-dwelling bird with spiky, grey-brown plumage. Longer body feathers bronze and black in colour. Face typically paler, with beady black eye and visible ear just behind it. Long whiskers at base of long, pinkish bill. Nostrils positioned close to bill-tip. Powerful stout legs scaled grey and tipped with black claws. Flightless like all kiwi with vestigial wings hidden beneath feathers. **DISTRIBUTION** Patchy, with subpopulations in Northland and Auckland, Coromandel Ranges to Bay of Plenty, W Waikato and Taranaki, and Te Urewera Ranges down to southern Hawke's Bay. Translocateed populations at Tawharanui in North Auckland, Maungatautari, Cape Kidnappers and Rimutaka Range. **HABITS AND HABITAT** Predominately nocturnal; found in native and exotic forest. Feeds on small invertebrates obtained by probing bill

into rotten log, leaf litter or soft earth. Usually lays two eggs per clutch with two clutches in a season, exclusively incubated by male. Male call a persistent, ascending whistle; female call more guttural. Duets heard throughout the night, year round. **CONSERVATION** Endemic/Not Threatened, with about 25,000 individuals. Heavily affected by dry summers in Northland; birds struggling to find food can be seen by day. Rearing of chicks in captivity or dedicated creches until rerelease as adults has allowed populations to grow in presence of predators, and establish new populations.

Adult (captive)

Adult

Rowi ■ *Apteryx rowi* 40–55cm ℮
(Okarito Brown Kiwi)

DESCRIPTION Soft, grey-brown plumage; streaked black on body. Some birds have whitish patches on face. Slender bill, stout legs and claws pale pinkish-grey. **DISTRIBUTION** Restricted to 11,000ha Okarito Forest in W coast, SI. Translocated to Mana Island north of Wellington, and Motuara and Blumine Islands in Marlborough Sounds. **HABITS AND HABITAT** Nocturnal, spending daylight in burrow or hollow log. Female lays up to three eggs in multiple nests, incubated by both sexes. Each egg is 20 per cent of female's body weight. Male gives piercing, high-pitched scream; female utters hoarser *brrr* call. **CONSERVATION** Endemic/Nationally Endangered. Once inhabited much vaster area of NZ.

Adult

Southern Brown Kiwi ■ *Apteryx australis* 45–65cm ℮
(tokoeka)

DESCRIPTION ssp. *australis* (Stewart Island), subsp. (South Island). Largest kiwi. Dull brown overall with streaked body feathers. Long, pale bill slightly downcurved. Strong legs and claws pale. **DISTRIBUTION** Subpopulations in Haast, Fiordland (Milford Sound to Preservation Inlet) and Rakiura/Stewart Island (plus Ulva Island). Introduced to Coal and Rarotoka Islands, and Orokonui Ecosanctuary, Dunedin. **HABITS AND HABITAT** Favours native forest, scrubland and beaches. Generally nocturnal; some birds forage throughout the day, especially further S. Rakiura/Stewart Island birds differ as they often congregate in big family groups with an alpha male and female. Male's call a shrill cry; female's a ghoulish shriek. **CONSERVATION** Endemic/Nationally Endangered. Intensive control of stoats across Fiordland has increased chick survival.

Chick

Adult

Little Spotted Kiwi ▪ *Apteryx owenii* 30–45cm
(kiwi pukupuku)

DESCRIPTION Smallest of the kiwi, with shaggy, warm-grey plumage forming mottled pattern across body. Like other kiwi, tiny vestigial wings sit under the feathers. Ear-coverts and iris dark, and relatively short narrow bill pinkish in colour with long whiskers (or vibrissae) at base. Scaling on legs light brown with white claws. **DISTRIBUTION** Once widespread throughout NZ, five birds from the dwindling population were placed on Kapiti Island in 1912, where they have expanded to around 1,300 individuals today. New populations have since been established on Taranga/Hen and Tiritiri Matangi Islands in the Hauraki Gulf, Red Mercury Island, Zealandia and Shakespear Sanctuaries, Long Island in the Marlborough Sounds, and Anchor and Chalky Islands in Fiordland. **HABITS AND HABITAT** Territories can cover many vegetation types, from native forest and scrub,

to flax and grassland. Pairs tend to mate for life, although divorces do happen. Usually one egg is laid per season, and it will only be incubated by the male. Chicks do not receive food from the parents, and leave the burrow roughly one week after hatching (before this they are nourished by the yolk sac). Main male call a series of shrill whistles, and female call is an ascending whirr sound. **CONSERVATION** Endemic/Nationally Increasing. At higher risk than other kiwi of disturbance from introduced mammals, which led to extinction on mainland.

Adult

Adult

Great Spotted Kiwi ■ *Apteryx maxima* 45–60cm
(roroa)

DESCRIPTION Large and robust kiwi with warm grey-brown plumage. Each feather has white banding and a dark tip, giving the bird a mottled appearance. Long, cream-coloured bill with nostrils at tip and sensitive whiskers (vibrissae) around gape. Females larger, with longer bill than males. Legs grey with dark claws. **DISTRIBUTION** Three major populations remain in the upper SI: Kahurangi National Park in north-west Nelson, the Paparoa Range in West Coast, and the Southern Alps centred around Arthur's Pass. Translocations to Nelson Lakes National Park commenced in 2004. **HABITS AND HABITAT** Occurs in damp beech forests with adequate ground cover in mountainous and subalpine regions, also using nearby tussock grassland. Flightless and nocturnal as are all kiwi, spending the day in a burrow, crevice or hollow log and emerging after dark to probe for invertebrates. Bonded pairs highly aggressive and make use of sharp claws to defend their territory against neighbouring birds. Most vocal of all kiwi: female's call a series of rising whistles, while male has a short, shrill warble. **CONSERVATION** Endemic/Nationally Vulnerable, population thought to be around 15,000 birds. The harsh environment it inhabits could result in a lower frequency of encounters with mammalian predators like dogs and stoats, which were responsible for the birds' historic disappearance from lowland areas. Chicks extremely prone to predation.

Adult

Adult

Mute Swan ■ *Cygnus olor* 130–160cm
(wāna)

Adult with goslings

DESCRIPTION Huge white swan with broad wings and long, curved neck. Bill reddish-orange with black base extending up to eye. Black knob on head, larger on male and during breeding. Immatures dirty white above with brown bill. Heaviest flying bird in NZ (males can reach 15kg), flying with neck outstretched. **DISTRIBUTION** Localized introduction scattered across mainland NZ in low numbers, with highest density around Christchurch. Native to Eurasia. **HABITS AND HABITAT** Favours large freshwater lakes and wetlands, feeding on bordering vegetation. Very territorial and can be aggressive when protecting nests and young. Despite its name, capable of grunts and hisses. **CONSERVATION** Introduced and naturalized.

Black Swan ■ *Cygnus atratus* 110–140cm
(kakīānau)

DESCRIPTION Unmistakable large swan with black plumage overall, excluding white wing feathers. Tertial feathers above tail curled. White-banded red bill extends up to orange iris. Webbed feet black. Pale-billed juveniles smoky-grey overall. Flies with neck outstretched. **DISTRIBUTION** Abundant across mainland NZ and Chatham Islands, after being introduced from Australia in 1864. Birds assumed to have naturally arrived as well, and could be considered a native species. **HABITS AND HABITAT** Resident of lakes and wetlands, as well as oxidation and farm ponds, and tidal estuaries. Nest a large mound constructed from aquatic plant matter. Completely herbivorous. Main call a descending *honk*. **CONSERVATION** Introduced and naturalized.

Juvenile

Adult

Canada Goose ■ *Branta canadensis* 75–100cm
(kuihi)

DESCRIPTION ssp. *maxima*. Distinctively marked goose. Body feathers grey-brown with light tips; cream breast cleanly separated from black neck and head. White patch extends from chin to ear-coverts. Tail and rump black, latter bordered white. Bill black and legs greyish. Goslings coated in dull yellow down. **DISTRIBUTION** Introduced to NZ in 1905 and now widespread over mainland. Native to North America; now introduced across much of northern hemisphere. **HABITS AND HABITAT** Occurs in large flocks on edges of freshwater lakes and open pastureland. Aggressive when nesting. Call a loud *honk*, given in flight or when alarmed. **CONSERVATION** Introduced and naturalized. Damages pasture and crops.

Greylag Goose ■ *Anser anser* 75–90cm
(kuihi)

DESCRIPTION Stocky goose. Wild form has grey-brown plumage going darker on flanks and upperwings; white underwings and lower belly. Heavy bill and strong legs bright orange. Feral domestic forms generally snowy-white or somewhere in between both plumages; stockier and stands more upright. Populations may revert to wild form over time. Juveniles smaller with lighter bill. **DISTRIBUTION** Fairly widespread across NI and SI. Native across Eurasia. **HABITS AND HABITAT** Commonly found in urban parks, freshwater lakes and pastureland. Gregarious bird, always encountered in flocks. Grazes on plant matter, sometimes far from water. Main call a series of quavering *honks*. **CONSERVATION** Introduced and naturalized.

Feral domestic form   Wild form

Cape Barren Goose ■ *Cereopsis novaehollandiae* 75–90cm

DESCRIPTION Stocky grey goose with white crown. Uniform grey spots and blotches cover back; wing edges and tail dark. Short bill pale green (darker in juveniles than adults), with drooping black tip. Iris dark brown, legs brick-red and feet black. **DISTRIBUTION** Highly localized; most regularly seen in Canterbury. First released in 1914, but today most birds reported are probably escapees. **HABITS AND HABITAT** Favours freshwater wetlands and adjacent damp pasture, grazing on exotic grasses. After mating, pairs perform a success display, facing each other, calling loudly and raising their heads repeatedly. Call a rattling *honk*. **CONSERVATION** Introduced and naturalized. Some records may even be naturally occurring vagrants.

Australian Wood Duck ■ *Chenonetta jubata* 45–50cm
(Maned Duck)

DESCRIPTION Small duck. Male pale grey with chocolate-brown head, dark 'mane' down nape, and buff blotching across breast. Speculum white with green bar. Flight feathers, belly and tail black. Small, stubby bill black; legs grey. Smaller female similar with pale

facial stripes, more muted plumage and more extensive blotching. **DISTRIBUTION** Vagrants from Australia, first recorded breeding in 2015 near Mapua in Nelson, have bred in every subsequent season and appear to be increasing (flock of 25 recorded). **HABITS AND HABITAT** Occurs in urban ponds and rural farm drains. Herbivorous, grazing on lawns adjacent to water. Male call an ascending hum; also gives a rising chatter. **CONSERVATION** Native/Colonizer.

Male (left) and female

Paradise Shelduck ■ *Tadorna variegata* 63–70cm ⓔ
(pūtangitangi)

DESCRIPTION Stocky, goose-like duck with extreme sexual dimorphism. Male has charcoal plumage, while female has white head and neck with chestnut over body. Wings of both sexes mostly white, with patches of black, metallic green and chestnut. Iris black; bill and legs dark grey. Juveniles resemble male; gradually lighten if female. Ducklings snow-white with brown blotches. **DISTRIBUTION** Abundant across mainland and large inshore islands. **HABITS AND HABITAT** Benefitted from European settlers clearing forests; now NZ's most widespread endemic bird. Favours urban parks, lakes, estuaries and open country. Pairs often bond for life and keenly defend territories. Diet mainly grasses and aquatic plants. Male call a *zip-zoop*-type honk. Females give shrill whine. **CONSERVATION** Endemic/Not Threatened.

Male

Female

Australian Shelduck ■ *Tadorna tadornoides* 55–72cm
(Chestnut-breasted Shelduck)

DESCRIPTION Much like NZ's local Paradise Shelduck (above). Mainly black plumage with white neck-rings, and orange-brown breast and wing markings. Large white patches and green iridescence adorn wings. Female has white around eyes and bill. Juveniles duller and lack neck-ring. **DISTRIBUTION** Irregular visitor to NZ with individuals reported most years. Invasions of up to 13 birds have occurred. One breeding record, at Lake Tekapo in 1985. Common throughout W and SE Australia. **HABITS AND HABITAT** Favours freshwater lagoons, coastal wetlands and pasture, where it can graze, dabble and filter-feed. Primarily herbivorous but also takes invertebrates. Nests usually in tree cavities lined with downy feathers. Call a deep honk. **CONSERVATION** Native/Vagrant.

Female

Whio ■ *Hymenolaimus malacorhynchos* 50–55cm ⓔ
(Blue Duck)

DESCRIPTION Iconic high-country duck. Plumage grey-blue overall; slightly darker on head. Breast marked chestnut, with brown wash over upperwings and tail. Faint green sheen on head and back more prominent on larger males. Iris bright yellow, and bill pale pink with black fleshy tip. Webbed feet and legs dark grey. Juveniles have duller plumage with uniform dark speckling on underside. **DISTRIBUTION** Scarce; ranges across NI from Mt Taranaki in W to Te Urewera in east, with bulk of population found on Central Plateau, a key site being the Turangi River. In SI focused around NW Nelson, West Coast and Fiordland. **HABITS AND HABITAT** Keeps mainly to remote forested areas, from sea level to subalpine zones. Specialist of clean, fast-flowing rivers and streams, from which it forages invertebrates with the aid of its fleshy bill-tip. In August, 5–6 pale eggs laid under thick vegetation. Fiercely aggressive towards interlopers, with territory being maintained by both birds year round. Male call a shrill whistle; female gives a low, husky grunt. **CONSERVATION** Endemic/Nationally Vulnerable. Mammalian predator attacks are common, with stoats particularly affecting adult birds, and rats their nests. Competes with introduced trout for food, and suffers from deterioration of habitat caused by vegetation removal, water pollution and hydroelectric dams.

Adult

Adult with ducklings

Grey Teal ▪ *Anas gracilis* 42–47cm
(tētē-moroiti)

DESCRIPTION Small, nondescript duck with mottled greyish plumage. Dark flecking covers rounded crown and continues down nape. White wing-panel and dark green speculum on upper wing evident in flight. Iris bright red, bill and legs slate-grey. Sexes alike. Australian vagrant **Chestnut Teal** *A. castanea* similar; male rich chestnut with dark green head. **DISTRIBUTION** Occurs widely across mainland NZ. Also resident in Australia, New Caledonia and New Guinea. **HABITS AND HABITAT** Gregarious; usually seen in large flocks on shallow freshwater lakes, wetlands, ponds and occasionally coastal mudflats. Diet of aquatic insects, foraged mainly at night. Male call a staccato laughter-like sound; also grunts and whistles. **CONSERVATION** Native/Not Threatened.

Brown Teal ▪ *Anas chlorotis* 48cm ⓔ
(pāteke)

DESCRIPTION Small duck with dark brown feathers with buff edging. Head unmarked apart from distinctive white eye-ring around black eye. Bill and legs slate-grey. Breeding male develops richer brown on breast, green on head, and faint white collar and flank-spot. Female and juveniles uniformly dull. **DISTRIBUTION** E coast of Northland, Hauturu/Little Barrier and Aotea/Great Barrier Island. Translocations to Auckland, Coromandel, Kapiti Island, Tasman and Fiordland doing well. South Island form extinct. **HABITS AND HABITAT** Found in freshwater wetland systems and estuaries. Diet of invertebrates, vegetation and fungi, foraged outside of daylight hours. Calls range from piping and whistling, to hoarse quacks and growls. **CONSERVATION** Endemic/Recovering. Bred in captivity for release in predator-free or controlled areas.

Adults

Breeding male

Auckland Island Teal ■ *Anas aucklandica* 45cm ⓔ
(tētē kākāriki)

DESCRIPTION Dumpy, flightless duck with dark brown plumage. Breeding male has green sheen on head and back, white eye-ring, reddish breast and fine barring across body. Underside of stumpy wings pale. Female similar to eclipse male with dull brown colouring overall. Bill slate-grey and legs olive-green. **DISTRIBUTION** Resident in

subantarctic Auckland Islands group except Auckland Island itself, due to presence of cats and rats. **HABITS AND HABITAT** Favours mega-herb fields, tussock grassland and adjacent streams, as well as shoreline among beach-cast kelp. Territories well protected from neighbouring pairs. Feeds mainly on crustaceans and invertebrates. Male's call a whirring whistle, compared to female's growl. **CONSERVATION** Endemic/ Nationally Vulnerable.

Adult pair

Campbell Island Teal ■ *Anas nesiotis* 43cm ⓔ

DESCRIPTION Smaller than relative teals. Dark brown overall with white eye-ring. Breeding male gains green tinge to sooty head, chestnut breast and pale patch near tail.

Flightless; short wings half of body length. **DISTRIBUTION** Restricted to subantarctic Campbell and Dent Islands, and introduced to Whenua Hou/Codfish Island. **HABITS AND HABITAT** Occurs along shoreline, peaty streams, and fields of tussock and mega-herbs, rarely venturing far from cover to fossick for amphipods and invertebrates. Known call a soft,

piping sound. **CONSERVATION** Endemic/Nationally Increasing. Small population rediscovered in 1973, then captive bred to increase numbers.

Breeding male

Mallard ▪ *Anas platyrhynchos* 50–65cm

DESCRIPTION ssp. *platyrhynchos*. Typical dabbling duck. Breeding male smart with shiny green head, white collar and yellow bill. Breast maroon; back pale grey; tail black with curled feathers. Non-breeding male subdued, and female mottled brown with duller bill. Speculum on wing blue with white edges. Legs bright orange. Many unusual plumage variants due to hybridization and origin of captive stock. **DISTRIBUTION** Introduced in 1870–1930. Abundant across NZ, as well as North America and Eurasia. **HABITS AND HABITAT** Never far from water, including parks, lowland lakes, rivers and estuaries. Readily interacts with humans for food. Call a simple *quack* and deep *wig-wig*. **CONSERVATION** Introduced and naturalized.

Female

Male

Grey Duck

▪ *Anas superciliosa* 50–60cm
(pārera, Pacific Black Duck)

DESCRIPTION ssp. *superciliosa*. Medium-sized duck. Face and throat cream with black crown and two black stripes; body dark brown with buff-edged feathers. Eye reddish, bill slate-grey and legs grey-brown. In flight, metallic green speculum and white underwing visible. Hybrids variable; can appear anywhere between Mallard (above) and Grey Duck. Less-defined facial stripes, greenish bill, blue speculum or orange legs give them away. **DISTRIBUTION** Sparse across mainland NZ and Chatham Islands. Also throughout Australia, Indonesia and Pacific. **HABITS AND HABITAT** Fairly wary, remaining largely in extensive wetlands and headwater catchments. Hybrids favour similar habitats to Mallards. **CONSERVATION** Native/Nationally Vulnerable. Disappearing from extensive hybridization, yet still legally hunted during waterfowl season in May–June.

Pure

Mallard hybrid

Male

Female

Australasian Shoveler

▪ *Spatula rhynchotis* 46–53cm
(kuruwhengi)

DESCRIPTION Low-sitting duck with distinctive shovel-shaped bill. Male has grey-blue head with pale crescent and black stripe before yellow eye. Flanks chestnut, layered with black spotting that continues on to breast (whitens in breeding plumage). Female speckled brown, darker above, and with brown iris. Green, blue and white wings seen in flight, and pale undersides. Orange legs stand out. **Northern Shoveler** *A. clypeata* a rare vagrant with white breast and dark green head. **DISTRIBUTION** Widespread across NZ. Also in Australia. **HABITS AND HABITAT** Occurs on freshwater lakes, oxidation ponds, sheltered estuaries and wetland areas. Forages with head below the surface, sifting through water or mud for aquatic invertebrates and plants. **CONSERVATION** Native/Not Threatened.

Male

Female

New Zealand Scaup

▪ *Aythya novaseelandiae* 40cm ⓔ
(pāpango)

DESCRIPTION Reminiscent of rubber duck on the water. Male brownish-black with green sheen across face, blue-grey bill and bright yellow eye. Plumage of female dull brown, with hazel iris and grey bill; usually has band of white feathers at base. Pale blotching on belly and distinctive white wing-panels of both sexes visible in flight. Similar **Australian White-eyed Duck** *A. australis* a rare vagrant. **DISTRIBUTION** Resident across NI and SI, bulk in Waikato, Bay of Plenty, Canterbury and Otago. **HABITS AND HABITAT** Typically found on expansive lakes and wetlands as well as some urban parks. Often congregates in large flocks with other waterfowl. Dives for up to 30 seconds in search of aquatic plants and insects. **CONSERVATION** Endemic/Not Threatened.

California Quail ■ *Callipepla californica* 25cm
(tikaokao)

DESCRIPTION ssp. *brunnescens*. Male brown above with cornflour-blue breast, nape and tail, white markings around black face and patterned belly. Plume shoots from chestnut crown of male. Plume smaller on female, which is grey-brown overall. Stubby bill and grey legs. Upright stance. Takes off with whirring wingbeats. **DISTRIBUTION** Widespread across NI and parts of SI; initially introduced in 1862. Natural range extends down W coast of North America. **HABITS AND HABITAT** Favours dry scrubland, open country and woodland, and rural gardens. Gregarious, feeding in covey on seeds, fruits and grains. Distinctive, three-note *uh-aah-uh* call and staccato clucking when alarmed. **CONSERVATION** Introduced and naturalized.

Female

Male

Chukar ■ *Alectoris chukar* 32–35cm

DESCRIPTION Plump, medium-sized partridge. Rusty-grey above with black stripe beginning above bill, extending through eye, forming collar across breast. Underside buff. Flanks boldly streaked black, white and rufous. Eye-ring, stout bill and legs cherry-red. Female slightly smaller than male. Prefers to run rather than fly. **DISTRIBUTION** Ranges throughout C SI from inland Marlborough to C Otago. Best viewing at Mt John Observatory near Tekapo. Introduced from C Asia in 1920s. **HABITS AND HABITAT** Mostly subalpine, favouring steep, dry hillsides with scattered vegetation. Wary in the open; forages in pairs or family groups for seeds and grains. Main call a repetitive, scratchy *chuck-uh-uh*. **CONSERVATION** Introduced and naturalized.

Brown Quail ▪ *Synoicus ypsilophorus* 18–20cm
(kuera)

DESCRIPTION ssp. *australis* (Australian). Plump, cryptically coloured quail. Male feathers chestnut to grey; lightly barred with black. Face and underside paler. Female darker with heavier black mottling, especially over back. Iris red, stubby bill slate-grey and legs bright

yellow. **DISTRIBUTION** Scattered from Northland to Bay of Plenty in small numbers after 1866 introduction; especially numerous in Shakespear and Tawharanui Regional Parks and on Hauraki Gulf Islands. Endemic to Australia and New Guinea. **HABITS AND HABITAT** Favours low-lying coastal scrub and farmland with sufficient vegetation. Diet of seed, leaves and invertebrates. Enjoys dust baths in sunny patches near cover. Gives range of shrill calls, including rising *ker-wee* used to bring covey members together. **CONSERVATION** Introduced and naturalized.

Male (right) and female

Common Pheasant ▪ *Phasianus colchicus* 55–90cm
(peihana)

DESCRIPTION Long-tailed gamebird. Male boasts iridescent green head with red facial skin and white collar. Body feathers strikingly patterned gold, orange and grey, and long, barred tail trailing behind. Female drab khaki with brown and black markings concentrated on back and crown. Generally horizontal but stands upright once alerted. **DISTRIBUTION** Widespread over mainland NZ in suitable areas; less common in SI. Native to Eurasia; first introduced in 1842. **HABITS AND HABITAT** Occurs in open country and scrubland.

Always close to cover, either disappearing into undergrowth or erupting into the air when disturbed. Diet of seeds, foliage and invertebrates. Call ranges from harsh clucking to loud, cough-like *kok-kok*. **CONSERVATION** Introduced and naturalized.

Male

Female

Indian Peafowl ■ *Pavo cristatus* 95–225cm
(pīkao)

DESCRIPTION Huge iconic pheasant. Male peacock velvet-blue with black and white barring on back and orange wings. Intricately patterned tail feathers to 140cm long, raised into distinctive fan shape while displaying, not unlike small crest adorning head. Smaller peahen drab brown above and pale below, with more extensive white facial skin; lacks impressive tail. **DISTRIBUTION** Locally common across NI and increasingly in Canterbury. Native to India and surrounds. **HABITS AND HABITAT** Resident of rough farmland and exotic forests. Most active around dawn and dusk, congregating in large flocks. Omnivorous. Male gives trumpeting *eow* call, most frequently in breeding season. **CONSERVATION** Introduced and naturalized.

Male

Female

Wild Turkey ■ *Meleagris gallopavo* 80–125cm
(korukoru)

DESCRIPTION ssp. *gallopavo* (Gould's). Distinctive for large body, long legs and disproportionately tiny bald blue head, covered in unsightly red caruncles (reduced in non-breeders and females), and wattle on bill (snood). Feathering mostly slate-grey with green sheen; wing feathers barred. Male's white-tipped tail fanned during displays. Female significantly smaller, with duller plumage. **DISTRIBUTION** First liberated in 1860s. Now fairly widespread across NI, and increasingly in SI. Native to North America. **HABITS AND HABITAT** Wary and gregarious bird of lowland open country, especially areas without intensive farming. Roosts in trees and on fence posts at night. Well-known *gobble-gobble* call. **CONSERVATION** Introduced and naturalized.

Male (right) and female

Australasian Crested Grebe ■ *Podiceps cristatus* 48–60cm
(pūteketeke, Great Crested Grebe)

DESCRIPTION ssp. *australis*. Large, long-necked bird with pointed pinkish bill, dark brown upperparts and white underparts. Adults unmistakable, with rufous cheek frills and head-crest. Juveniles grey with black and white facial stripes. **DISTRIBUTION** Restricted to SI, with greatest numbers in C Canterbury and Otago. Also throughout Africa and Eurasia, and in Australia. **HABITS AND HABITAT** Well-vegetated shallow lakes from coastal wetlands to high country. Well known for ceremonial courtship display, including head shaking, plant offerings and spectacular feat of walking on water. Feeds predominately on fish. Call a far-reaching growl. **CONSERVATION** Native/Nationally Vulnerable; low population despite being common overseas. Recreational boats can cause disturbance to nests and pairs.

Adult pair

New Zealand Dabchick ■ *Poliocephalus rufopectus* 28–30cm ⓔ
(weweia, New Zealand Grebe)

DESCRIPTION Small, blackish-brown grebe with pale yellow eyes and fine silver feathers across face. Reddish breast and neck fade in non-breeding plumage. Cream-coloured underparts larger in immature birds, and young have striped facial markings. Stands out for long neck and pointed black bill. **DISTRIBUTION** Widespread but sparse across NI. Rare in SI, breeding at the top. **HABITS AND HABITAT** Found on freshwater lakes, dams and farm ponds. As in all grebes, 'lobed' feet efficiently propel and steer it underwater. After breeding, birds flock to more open waterbodies. Aquatic invertebrates are preferred prey. Rarely vocal. **CONSERVATION** Endemic/Nationally Increasing. Threats include drainage of wetlands and dwindling riparian vegetation.

Adult with chick

Hoary-headed Grebe ■ *Poliocephalus poliocephalus* 29cm

(taihoropī)

DESCRIPTION Greyish upperparts and cream underneath; separated from similar New Zealand Dabchick (opposite) by overall paler plumage, brown iris and heavier white-tipped bill. Grebe tails are little more than a small tuft. Breeding adults have entirely black heads featuring streaky white feathers across face and crown. **DISTRIBUTION** Rare visitor from SE Australia, but since 2018 multiple pairs have bred at Lake Elterwater in Marlborough. **HABITS AND HABITAT** Frequents areas of large, open water, such as lakes, ponds and estuaries. Dense waterproof plumage aids buoyancy from air bubbles trapped underneath feathers. This can be regulated, allowing it to deep dive in search of aquatic arthropods. Seldom vocalizes but chatters within pairs or when alarmed. **CONSERVATION** Native/Colonizer.

Breeding adult

Australasian Little Grebe ■ *Tachybaptus novaehollandiae* 25–27cm

(tokitokipio)

DESCRIPTION ssp. *novaehollandiae*. Smallest of four grebes in NZ, with yellow skin-patch at base of black bill. Chestnut-coloured stripe on neck, running down in crescent from glossy-black head. Non-breeding birds pale grey below. **DISTRIBUTION** Self-introduced in 1977 from Australia; small breeding population now exists in Northland and North Auckland. Vagrant to rest of mainland. **HABITS AND HABITAT** Confined to freshwater wetlands. Creates floating nests of aquatic vegetation to 60cm high. Young often ride on parents' backs, characteristic of all grebes. Effective at long-distance dispersal but rarely seen in flight. Often dives when disturbed, or when preying on small fish and insects. **CONSERVATION** Native/Colonizer.

Pair at nest

Long-tailed Cuckoo ■ *Eudynamys taitensis* 40–42cm ⓔ
(koekoeā)

DESCRIPTION Large, cryptic-coloured cuckoo with very long, white-tipped tail, effectively doubling its length. Dark brown above with orange mottling, and off-white below with brown striations across breast and face. Orange and brown barring runs length of tail. Hooked, ivory-coloured bill, and brown eye. Juveniles have cinnamon wash over underside, and are more intensely marked. Rarely seen except in flight, high and fast across an open space. **DISTRIBUTION** Summer migrant, present in September–March. Breeds only in NZ, across NI, SI and Rakiura/Stewart Islands (and some offshore islands such as Hauturu/Little Barrier). Winters in Pacific; mainly Fiji and Society Islands. **HABITS AND HABITAT** Occurs in mature native forest as well as exotic pine plantations, spending most of its time concealed in the canopy. Brood parasite, favouring the Whitehead (p. 147) in NI, Mohua (p. 146) and Brown Creeper (p. 147) in S, laying one pale pink egg in their nests. Opportunistic feeder, taking leaves, berries, insects and even small birds. Call loud and piercing, an escalating, drawn-out shriek usually repeated every few seconds. Can be heard any time of day or night. Call often the only way to detect it. **CONSERVATION** Endemic/Nationally Vulnerable. May be linked to decline in host species and habitat loss in Pacific Islands. Have not yet recolonized any sites Whiteheads have been reestablished, as they prefer to return to site of origin.

Adult

Shining Cuckoo ■ *Chalcites lucidus* 15–17cm
(pīpīwharauroa, Shining Bronze-cuckoo)

DESCRIPTION ssp. *lucidus*. Small cuckoo with distinctive iridescent bronze-green upperparts, and similarly coloured barring across white breast and belly. Face pale with dark flecking; undertail grey with white blotches. Male has greenish crown; female's has faint purple tinge. Iris dark brown; slender bill and stubby legs black. Immatures told by softer plumage and pinkish bill. **DISTRIBUTION** Summer migrant generally arriving from September. Breeds across NI, SI, Stewart Island and Chatham Islands, as well as adjacent offshore islands, before leaving again in March. Wintering birds reside between New Guinea and Solomon Islands. Elsewhere breeds in Australia, Vanuatu and New Caledonia. **HABITS AND HABITAT** Although rarely seen, fairly common in suburban areas: parks, gardens and small patches of bush, in addition to larger tracts of native forest. Brood parasite, primarily affecting Grey and Chatham Island Warblers (p. 139), and occasionally other small bird species. Lays single grey egg; once hatched, cuckoo chick evicts any other eggs or chicks in nest. Warbler host then raises cuckoo as its own. Diet mostly of invertebrates such as caterpillars. Distinctive call a rising whistle repeated 5–10 times at once, capped with 2–3 descending notes. **CONSERVATION** Native/ Not Threatened. Like other cuckoos, often victim of window strikes.

Juvenile

Adult

Adult

Kererū

▪ *Hemiphaga novaeseelandiae* 51cm ⓔ
(New Zealand Pigeon)

DESCRIPTION Chunky, small-headed pigeon with shiny plumage over head, breast and wings that consists of a variety of greens and purples with bronze tinge. White on belly cleanly separated at breast; continues up over shoulders reminiscent of a singlet. Small bill orange-red (tipped black on immature birds) and iris red. Flight feathers dark with grey accents. Underwings pale, rump greenish and tail dark grey with lighter tips, grey with a dark band underneath. Feet brick-red. Very loud flier, with noise caused by air passing by wings. **DISTRIBUTION** Resident throughout NI and SI, Rakiura/Stewart Island and forested offshore islands. Uncommon in C SI plains and alpine areas. **HABITS AND HABITAT** Found primarily in native forest but also increasingly in urban parks and gardens. Due to size and preference for eating fruits of native trees, considered an important disperser of seeds in forest ecosystems. Also commonly takes flowers, buds and leaves. Incredible aerial displays with steep climbs and dives can be seen year round. Call a soft *coo*, seldom heard. **CONSERVATION** Endemic/Not Threatened. Predation by feral cats, possums, stoats and rats impacts population levels; marked increase in pest-free zones. Occasionally falls victim to vehicle and window strikes.

Adult

Immature

Parea ▪ *Hemiphaga chathamensis* 55cm ⓔ
(Chatham Island Pigeon)

DESCRIPTION Enormous pigeon, heavier and bulkier than mainland cousin. Dark grey-blue on head, breast and wings, and purple over back. White belly continues to shoulders. Two-toned bill red with bulbous yellow tip. Rump grey and tail dark. Loud whirring wings in flight. **DISTRIBUTION** Once found throughout Chatham Islands, but now remains only in S corner of Rēkohu/Chatham Island itself. **HABITS AND HABITAT** Favours native forest as well as rough pasture, foraging for leaves, flowers, berries, grasses and clovers. Call a soft *coo* seldom heard. **CONSERVATION** Endemic/Nationally Vulnerable. Key threat is predation by feral cats, possums, rats and Weka (p. 35).

Rock Pigeon ▪ *Columba livia* 31–34cm
(kererū aropari)

DESCRIPTION The city bird – familiar plump pigeon with variable plumage. 'Wild-type' birds grey overall; wings paler with two black bands across them. Feral variants include entirely black, white and brown individuals. Iridescent purple and green on neck. Small, dark bill with white cere, orange eye and stubby reddish legs. **DISTRIBUTION** Resident across NI and SI close to human habitation. Occurs nearly worldwide. **HABITS AND HABITAT** Nests naturally on cliff faces but has adapted to tall buildings in cities (where it is undesirable, yet most often encountered). Also common in pastureland and rural areas. Eats mainly seeds, grains and food scraps. Call a low, rolling *coo*. **CONSERVATION** Introduced and naturalized. Originated from domesticated birds.

Wild-type variant

Feral variant

Barbary Dove ■ *Streptopelia risoria* 28cm

DESCRIPTION Domestic form of the **African-collared Dove** *S. roseogrisea*. Cream overall with narrow black neck-collar, edged white in male. Back and wings khaki with darker flight feathers; underside of tail black tipped white. Slender bill black, iris deep red and legs pink. Paler juveniles often lack collar completely. **DISTRIBUTION** NZ population, derived from escaped and released birds, found in Northland, Auckland and Hawke's Bay, with smaller scattered populations still increasing in range. **HABITS AND**

HABITAT Confiding dweller of suburban parks and gardens. Feeds on seeds and cereal crops. Breeding male displays with the 'bow-coo' combo, inflating its chest to females. Hooting call can be rendered as *coo-kikiki-oo*. **CONSERVATION** Introduced and naturalized.

Spotted Dove ■ *Streptopelia chinensis* 32cm

DESCRIPTION ssp. *tigrina*. Long-tailed dove with greyish-pink head and underside. Thick black collar around back of neck covered in white spots. Back and wings fawn spotted brown. Flight feathers dark brown. Vent and outer-tail feathers white. Small bill black,

iris dull orange and legs brick-red. **DISTRIBUTION** Fairly common in upper NI; still increasing since introduction in 1920s. Native range SE Asia. **HABITS AND HABITAT** Readily found in suburban parks and gardens across range. Flight display performed by advertising male, climbing high in sky before gliding down in spiralling fashion with outspread wings and tail. Ground forager; diet mostly seeds and grains. Call a whistling *croo-croo*. **CONSERVATION** Introduced and naturalized.

Weka ■ *Gallirallus australis* 46–60cm ⓔ

DESCRIPTION ssp. *greyi* (North Island), *australis* (Western), *hectori* (Buff), *scotti* (Stewart Island). Iconic flightless rail with brown-streaked black feathering that varies considerably across range. Birds in N russet-brown, but can be almost entirely black in S. Most have mid-grey plumage on belly, throat and face to some extent, including bold eye-stripe. Pointed bill dull pink with dark tip, and eye deep red. Short, rounded wings and tail feathers strongly barred with black. Powerful legs grey to red. Sexes alike, except male larger than female. Immature birds have brown iris, black bill and darker plumage overall. Chicks covered in sooty-black down. **DISTRIBUTION** Sparse; bulk of population spread from West Coast to Marlborough Sounds, and Fiordland, Rakiura/Stewart Island and Rēkohu/Chatham Islands (introduced). Also on Kawau, Waiheke and Kapiti Islands further N, and pockets in Gisborne, Bay of Plenty and Northland.

HABITS AND HABITAT Very curious and inspective of humans. Occurs in range of environments, from native and exotic forests to open pasture, around coast, in wetlands and in alpine areas. Omnivorous diet, taking fruit, invertebrates, lizards, eggs, birds and mammals; scavenges carrion. In one year, can raise up to four broods, each consisting of four eggs if food is bountiful. Repertoire a series of piercing *coo-et*s and soft *ik-ik-ik* between birds. **CONSERVATION** Endemic/Not Threatened.

Stewart Island subspecies

Buff subspecies

Banded Rail ■ *Gallirallus philippensis* 30–33cm
(moho pererū, Buff Banded Rail)

DESCRIPTION ssp. *assimilis*. Striking rail. Olive-brown plumage above mottled black and white. Eye-stripe separates dark crown from chestnut face, pale grey chin and throat. Black and white barring extends across chest down to belly, with bold buff breast-band. Bill pinkish, iris deep red and legs grey. Juveniles duller than adults, with darker bill and legs. **DISTRIBUTION** Common coastally around upper NI and Nelson/Tasman. Widespread

from Australia to the Philippines. **HABITS AND HABITAT** Rarely far from mangroves and saltmarsh, apart from offshore islands, where it is considerably more tame, venturing on to lawns (most notably Aotea/Great Barrier Island). Feeds close to cover on range of invertebrates. Call reminiscent of a rusty gate. **CONSERVATION** Native/Declining.

Adult (right) and immature

Auckland Island Rail ■ *Lewinia muelleri* 20cm ⓔ

DESCRIPTION Small, short-winged rail. Plumage brown above turning rufous on neck and head. Wings, flanks and rump barred black and white, and throat and breast warm grey. Iris hazel, lores black; wedge-shaped bill pink, darker towards tip. Legs flesh coloured. Sexes similar although bill longer in male than female. Juveniles have more muted plumage, and downy chicks black. **DISTRIBUTION** Endemic to subantarctic Auckland Islands. Only known from Adams and Disappointment Islands within group. **HABITS AND HABITAT** Rarely seen due to highly secretive nature and dense mega-herb vegetation it inhabits. Call a loud hoarse, repeated *krek*. **CONSERVATION** Endemic/Naturally Uncommon. With a range-restricted population of around 1,500 birds, any diseases or predator incursions could prove disastrous.

Spotless Crake ▪ *Zapornia tabuensis* 17–20cm
(pūweto)

DESCRIPTION ssp. *tabuensis*. Tiny rail with bold red eye ringed in orange. Two-tone plumage with dark brown across back and wings; head and underparts slate-grey. Pointed bill black; undertail barred and legs pink. Duller immature birds paler in front. **DISTRIBUTION** Widespread over NI, adjacent offshore islands and Kermadec Islands. Rare in SI. Also found across Australia, Indonesia and SW Pacific. **HABITS AND HABITAT** Freshwater bird of lakes, wetlands and small ponds with sufficient cover. Those resident on offshore islands also enter native forest. Feeds on invertebrates mainly at dawn and dusk. Indicating call a series of *kreks* and whirring sound reminiscent of alarm clock. **CONSERVATION** Native/Declining.

Immature   *Adult*

Marsh Crake ▪ *Zapornia pusilla* 15–18cm
(kotoreke, Baillon's Crake)

DESCRIPTION ssp. *affinis*. Very small rail with cryptic plumage. Brown upperparts marked black and white, and blue-grey over breast and face. Black and white barring continues from flanks to undertail. Short bill green towards base, eyes bright red. **DISTRIBUTION** Widespread across NI and SI, more numerous further S. Elsewhere found across Australia and Eurasia. **HABITS AND HABITAT** Favours wetlands, lake and river verges, and saltmarsh habitats. Impressive disperser, but rarely seen due to inconspicuous nature and dense vegetation it frequents. Diet primarily invertebrates; known to feed throughout the night. Call a staccato *ke-ke-ke-ke-ke* interspersed with *krek*. **CONSERVATION** Native/ Declining. Ongoing habitat loss: 90 per cent of NZ wetlands have already been drained.

Adult   *Immature*

Australian Coot ■ *Fulica atra* 35–39cm
(Eurasian Coot)

DESCRIPTION ssp. *australis*. Dumpy aquatic rail. Glossy charcoal-grey plumage darker on head contrasts with white bill and frontal shield. Deep red iris, short, rounded wings and grey legs with lobed feet. Juveniles have smaller shield and paler on face and breast. Chicks bizarre, with multicoloured red, blue and orange heads. Rarely seen in flight; instead skims the water's surface. **DISTRIBUTION** Self-introduced from Australia, first breeding in NZ

in 1957. Now widespread across mainland in modest numbers. Other subspecies in Europe, N Africa and Asia. **HABITS AND HABITAT** Creates anchored floating nest of twigs and weeds. Inhabitant of large, well-vegetated lakes and wetlands. Call an explosive *tick*. **CONSERVATION** Native/Naturally Uncommon.

Adult and chick

Pūkeko ■ *Porphyrio melanotus* 44–48cm
(Australasian Swamphen)

DESCRIPTION ssp. *melanotus*. Lanky, long-legged rail with vivid blue underparts, and black head, back, wings and tail. Bill and large frontal shield bright red, with crimson iris, pale orange legs and long toes. Undertail-coverts white. Sexes similar, female smaller than male. Juveniles have darker plumage that colours up with age. Prefers to run when disturbed but a capable fliers once airborne. **DISTRIBUTION** Widespread across lowland areas of NI and SI (including adjacent islands), Rēkohu/Chatham Islands and Kermadec Islands. Also resident in Australia, New Guinea and E Indonesia. **HABITS AND HABITAT** Prefers less dry regions; often found near water, around freshwater lakes and

streams, wetlands, tidal harbours and estuaries, damp pastureland and urban parks. Family situation complicated. While birds do form monogamous pairs, they also form 'helper groups' of multiple adults to raise young. Females lay 4–6 brown spotted eggs in a clutch, but when several contribute to one nest, total can reach 18. Highly territorial; aggressive interactions and displays between neighbouring groups to flaunt size and frontal shield not uncommon. Opportunistic diet of grasses, insects and sometimes small birds and mammals. Familiar call like a piercing *honk*. Also gives softer *hiccup* and squawking calls. **CONSERVATION** Native/Not Threatened.

South Island Takahē ■ *Porphyrio hochstetteri* 63cm ⓔ

DESCRIPTION Bulky, flightless rail – the largest in the world. Upperparts mossy-green with turquoise trim to rounded wings, blending into dark blue head and underside. Undertail-coverts white. Huge brick-red bill and frontal shield distinctive. Stout orange legs. Sexes alike, smaller juveniles appear sooty overall with blackish bills. **DISTRIBUTION** Entire population became restricted to Murchison Mountains in Fiordland in 1900s. Introduced to various wildlife sanctuaries, including Tawharanui Regional Park, Tiritiri Matangi and Motutapu Islands in Auckland; Kapiti and Mana Islands near Wellington; and Maud Island in Marlborough Sounds. Second mainland population established in 2018 in Kahurangi National Park, NW SI. **HABITS AND HABITAT** Remnant population lives in environment comprising predominately alpine tussock grasses. Diet of grains and grasses but takes protein opportunistically in form of insects and small animals. Call a far-travelling *honk*, but also gives quiet *hoot* and deep, resonant *boom* indicative of alarm. **CONSERVATION** Endemic/Nationally Vulnerable. Recovering from supposed 50-year period of extinction after rediscovery in 1948 on mission led by Geoffrey Orbell. Captive breeding programme and translocation work resulted in population exceeding 400 birds in 2019 for the first time in over a century. Highly susceptible to predation from stoats.

Adult

Adult

Juvenile

Black morph

Variable Oystercatcher

■ *Haematopus unicolor* 47–49cm ⓔ
(tōrea pango)

DESCRIPTION Large wader with robust orange bill and pinkish legs. Plumage comes in three morphs: entirely black, pied (with white belly) and intermediate (or smudgy). Wings black with white wing-bar on pied-phase birds. Iris vivid red with orange ring. Juveniles have stouter, dark-tipped bills and pale feather edges. **DISTRIBUTION** Resident around NZ coast. Black morph occurs more frequently further S. **HABITS AND HABITAT** Strictly coastal, preferring sandy beaches, dunes, shell banks and rocky shores. Sedentary, resting in same area year round. Diet of crustaceans, worms, and molluscs that are opened by wedging bill into shell and twisting. Call a sharp *ki-woo* complemented by rapid, peeping calls. **CONSERVATION** Endemic/Recovering.

Intermediate morph

South Island Pied Oystercatcher ■ *Haematopus finschi* 46cm **e**
(tōrea)

DESCRIPTION Black and white wader with long, narrow bill. Head, breast and wings black; cleanly separated from white belly, which continues up to shoulders. Wings black with prominent white bar. Rump and tail white, the latter tipped black. Bill orange-red with dark tip in basic plumage. Eye red with orange ring, legs pinkish. Juveniles appear dull with lighter bills. **DISTRIBUTION** Breeds inland across eastern SI, wintering along coast of NI and SI. Vagrant to Australia. **HABITS AND HABITAT** Nests in colonies on farmland and riverbeds, moving to sheltered inlets and estuaries, where it feeds and roosts in immense flocks. Call a high-pitched *ki-woo*, as well as rapid piping whistles when alarmed. **CONSERVATION** Endemic/Not Threatened.

Chatham Island Oystercatcher
■ *Haematopus chathamensis* 47–49cm **e**
(tōrea tai)

DESCRIPTION Stocky wader with long orange bill. Head, breast, back and tail black. Smudgy white belly continues up to shoulders. Upperwings black with white bar; underwings white with dirty black border. Eye red with orange ring, legs pinkish. **DISTRIBUTION** Restricted to Rēkohu/Chatham Islands; on Chatham, Pitt, Rangatira and Māngere Islands and Star Keys. **HABITS AND HABITAT** Occurs along sandy and rocky coastlines, where birds defend territories year round. Call a hoarse *ki-woo* and piping whistles when alarmed. Can live for more than 30 years. **CONSERVATION** Endemic/Nationally Critical. Storm events and predation by introduced cats are biggest threats. Despite this, population has increased to over 300 individuals from a low of 50 in the 1970s.

Pied Stilt ▪ *Himantopus himantopus* 33–36cm
(poaka)

DESCRIPTION ssp. *leucocephalus*. Distinctive wader with needle-like black bill and extraordinarily long pink legs. Adult plumage mostly white with glossy black on nape, and pointed black wings. Eye red, and sexes similar. Legs extend far beyond tail in flight. Immature birds have dark patch on face; juveniles have mottled grey-brown feathering over wings and crown, shorter greyish bill and pale legs. 'Pied-like' Pied x Black Stilt (opposite) hybrids can be distinguished by their black neck collar; its broadness generally corresponds with level of Black Stilt genes. More typical birds have variable black mottling across head and body. **DISTRIBUTION** Widespread across NI and SI, as well as Chatham Islands, both inland and coastal. Also across Australasia; other forms worldwide. **HABITS AND HABITAT** Conspicuous bird that feeds in sizeable loose flocks on tidal mudflats in harbours and estuaries, lagoon and lake verges, and braided riverbeds. Highly territorial during breeding season, defending nest against perceived threats. Lays 3–4 well-

camouflaged eggs in mess of debris and mud. Parents may pretend to have an injured wing or leg to lure threats away. Diet of terrestrial and aquatic invertebrates. Prey caught primarily by sight, but also probes into shallow water or mud. Call a high-pitched yapping. **CONSERVATION** Native/Not Threatened.

Hybrid   *Immature*

Adult

Kakī ■ *Himantopus novaezelandiae* 37–40cm ⓔ
(Black Stilt)

DESCRIPTION Large, glossy black wader with pointed wings and tail. Named for very long, slender pink legs. Thin black bill slightly upturned. In sunlight plumage reveals metallic green shine. Juveniles mostly white with dull black on wings and face, similar to immatures, which gain peppered black feathering over white. Almost all pure individuals have unique colour-band combination. 'Black-like' Black x Pied Stilt (opposite) hybrids usually have white speckling on vent and belly, and at bill-base. **DISTRIBUTION** Breeding grounds have reduced over last century, with Mackenzie Basin in C SI remaining. During winter birds occasionally visit SI coastline, and rarely NI. **HABITS AND HABITAT** Pairs typically settle to breed in areas with abundant food, along braided riverbeds and in nearby wetlands. Four eggs laid in depression or clump of vegetation.

Carnivorous; adapted to feed on minute aquatic invertebrates such as molluscs, crustaceans and insect larvae. Call a single or repeated *yep*. **CONSERVATION** Endemic/ Nationally Critical. Threatened by hybridization with Pied Stilt, habitat loss to agricultural land and predation from introduced mammals. Captive breeding initiatives and intensive predator control in place to support wild populations, where around 200 adults remain.

Hybrid

Juvenile

Adult

Pacific Golden Plover ■ *Pluvialis fulva* 23–26cm
(kuriri)

DESCRIPTION Dainty plover; mottled black and gold above. Non-breeding plumage has light golden wash (brightest on juveniles) with brown streaking, and pale face and

belly. Striking breeding birds black on face and underside, with broad white band reaching from crown to shoulders. Underwings greyish. Stumpy bill black; long legs grey. **DISTRIBUTION** Regular summer visitor to NZ. Breeds across Siberia, moving to Australasia outside of breeding. **HABITS AND HABITAT** Bird of tidal estuaries and

lagoons, roosting on nearby shell banks, saltmarsh and grassland. About 300–500 individuals spend Sep–Apr season in NZ, and a few overwinter. Rarely allows for close approach while local. Call a disyllabic yelp. **CONSERVATION** Native/Migrant.

Non-breeding adult　　*Breeding adult*

Grey Plover ■ *Pluvialis squatarola* 27–30cm
(Black-bellied Plover)

DESCRIPTION Bulky, long-legged plover. Basic plumage dull grey with faint spotting above, and white face and belly. Large black axillary patch under wings diagnostic, visible in flight or while stretching. Rarely encountered locally in breeding plumage,

black below with white border and checkered black and white upperparts. Heavy bill black and legs grey. **DISTRIBUTION** One visits NZ most summers, often Kaipara Harbour or Farewell Spit. Breeds in Arctic Circle and occurs more or less worldwide. **HABITS AND HABITAT** Prefers sandy beaches and sheltered tidal mudflats. Diet of crustaceans, molluscs and marine worms, usually caught by sight, hence the large eyes. Call a piercing yelp. **CONSERVATION** Native/Vagrant.

Non-breeding adult

Wrybill ■ *Anarhynchus frontalis* 20–21cm ⓔ
(ngutu pare)

DESCRIPTION Small plover with stone-grey upperparts and white underparts. Unique in being the only bird in the world with bill bent to the side, specifically to the right. Male in breeding plumage gains black breast-band (thinner on female) and dark forehead with white front. Bent bill black and fairly long. Juveniles appear paler with straighter bill. **DISTRIBUTION** Breeding restricted to inland Canterbury and Otago, SI; birds then migrate to coasts of both main islands during winter, with hotspots being Manukau Harbour in Auckland and Pūkorokoro/Miranda. **HABITS AND HABITAT** Nests exclusively on braided riverbeds, relying on impressive camouflage to avoid detection. Clutch of two stone-like eggs laid in shallow scrape. Tiny chicks hatch after one month, and freeze when faced with potential threat. In off season, adults favour mudflats of harbours and inlets, roosting in flocks on adjacent shell banks and beaches. Often reacts with curiosity towards nearby humans. Bill specialized in scything under stones for small aquatic invertebrates and larvae. Main call a persistent, rising *weep* in addition to an antagonistic *chirring* sound for unwanted visitors. **CONSERVATION** Endemic/Nationally Increasing, with estimated population of 5,000 birds. Takeover of braided riverbeds by weeds, agricultural land and flooding is impacting breeding success.

Non-breeding adult

Breeding adult

New Zealand Dotterel ■ *Charadrius obscurus* 26–28cm Ⓔ
(tūturiwhatu, Red-breasted Plover)

DESCRIPTION ssp. *aquilonius* (Northern), *obscurus* (Southern). Stocky plover with thick black bill. Grey-brown above and white below, with bold eyebrow-stripe. Breeding birds develop orange flush over breast and belly, deeper on males and especially on darker southern subspecies (also gaining richer tones on back). Relatively short grey legs. Juveniles paler with white-edged feathers. Sand-coloured chicks resemble bumblebees on stilts. **DISTRIBUTION** Two genetically distinct populations. Northern subspecies found along coasts of Northland, Auckland, Waikato, Bay of Plenty and Gisborne, with birds occasionally seen further S. Nominate southern subspecies breeds inland on Rakiura/ Stewart Island, migrating to coast and Southland in winter, with key site being Awarua Bay. **HABITS AND HABITAT** Favours sandy beaches and shell banks, constructing nest

(simple scrape in the ground) on ridge above high-tide mark in which 1–3 dark-spotted brown eggs are laid. Chicks precocial, fledging after 5–6 weeks. Crustaceans, molluscs and invertebrates are main prey items. Main call a short trill; undulating territorial call. **CONSERVATION** Endemic/Recovering. Nesting habitat and season clash with activities of holiday makers, causing disturbance to adults and young. Storm events and predation also have major impact.

Non-breeding adult, Northern subspecies

Breeding adult, Northern subspecies

Breeding adult, Southern subspecies

Banded Dotterel

◼ *Charadrius bicinctus* 18–21cm ⓔ
(pohowera, Double-banded Plover)

Breeding adult

DESCRIPTION ssp. *bicinctus*, *excilis* (Auckland Island). Small plover with large head and attractive plumage; brown above with white on face and undersides. Large eye and small black bill; legs grey to yellow. Breeding birds darken around face and collar, and gain bold crimson breast-band. Juveniles similar to non-breeders but with paler tones over face and back. **DISTRIBUTION** Widespread across mainland; also on Chathams. Inland breeders migrate to coast until winter, some as far as Australia. **HABITS AND HABITAT** Nests from subalpine to sea level on braided riverbeds, grassland and beaches. Diet of crustaceans, worms and invertebrates. Main call a *wit-wit* interspersed with sharp peeps. **CONSERVATION** Endemic/Nationally Vulnerable. Human disturbance and predation while nesting are major threats.

Non-breeding adult

Greater Sand Plover ◼ *Charadrius leschenaultii* 24cm

DESCRIPTION ssp. *leschenaultii*. Superficially resembles the New Zealand Dotterel (opposite) but has slighter build, longer legs and more horizontal posture. Smooth grey-brown above with defined shoulder-tabs, white wing-bars, large eyes and heavy bill. Breeding birds develop chestnut colouring on head and breast and black mask. Extreme care must be taken to distinguish it from the rarer **Lesser Sand Plover** C. *mongolus*, which has slightly smaller bill and shorter, paler legs. **DISTRIBUTION** Up to five birds visit NZ in most years. Breeds C Asia; widespread from Africa to Australasia. **HABITS AND HABITAT** Forages for small worms and crustaceans on mudflats, sandspits and estuaries. Trilling call. **CONSERVATION** Native/Vagrant.

Breeding adult

Non-breeding adult

Shore Plover ■ *Thinornis novaseelandiae* 20cm ℯ
(tūturuatu, tchūriwat' in Moriori)

DESCRIPTION Small, handsome wader with lightly streaked brown on wings, tail, back and crown, white headband and underparts, and black head that is glossier on male than female. Darker outer upperwings interrupted by broad white wing-bar, and underwings clean white. Bill orange-red with black tip, appearing smudged on female. Eye-ring matches bill-base in colour, and legs pale orange. Juveniles have brown face, bold white supercilium and mostly dark bill. Stocky build with long, pointed wings, and direct flight style. **DISTRIBUTION** Disappeared from mainland NZ in 1800s and became restricted to South East Island in Rēkohu/ Chatham Island group. Translocations commencing in 2000s successful in establishing populations on Motutapu Island in Hauraki Gulf, and Waikawa Island in Hawke's Bay. Efforts still being made to keep birds at sites as they tend to disperse soon after release. **HABITS AND HABITAT** Diet of invertebrates, crustaceans and molluscs. Prefers to construct nests underneath driftwood or vegetation, seemingly for better protection from aerial predators. Intermittent piping and *seep*s make up call repertoire. **CONSERVATION** Endemic/ Nationally Critical. A single rat or stoat has proven to be capable of decimating an entire island's worth of birds. Total population about 250 individuals, up from 150 in 1990s; due to intensive management and captive-breeding programmes, continuing to increase.

Female

Male

Black-fronted Dotterel ■ *Elseyornis melanops* 16–18cm

DESCRIPTION Very small, dainty plover. Adults striking with brown-streaked crown and wings, and white underparts. Bold black 'V' on chest connects at nape with black facial stripe and forehead. White spot sits above red-ringed eye, and bill red tipped black. Tail and wing-bar chestnut. Toothpick-like legs orange. Juveniles lack black chest-band and are duller overall. **DISTRIBUTION** Still expanding. Presently occurs in small pockets throughout NI and SI; hotspots include Hawke's Bay, Wairarapa and Canterbury. **HABITS AND HABITAT** Commonly encountered on braided rivers, brackish freshwater wetlands and coastal mudflats, where it forages for small invertebrates along the water's edge. Main call a high, rapid *wit-wit-wit*. **CONSERVATION** Native/Naturally Uncommon.

Adult

Masked Lapwing ■ *Vanellus miles* 38cm
(Spur-winged Plover)

DESCRIPTION ssp. *novaehollandiae* (Black-shouldered). Large, brown and white wader with black crown, nape and shoulder-tabs. Bill and eye yellow, encompassed by triangular yellow wattle. Underwings and rump white; flight feathers and tail black (tipped white). Yellow spur juts from each shoulder. Legs long and blackish-red. Juveniles have mottled back and crown, smaller wattles and grey legs. **DISTRIBUTION** First bred in Southland in 1932; since expanded to be common across NZ including Chatham Islands. Elsewhere in Australia and New Guinea. **HABITS AND HABITAT** Widespread, favouring coastal or modified environments. Bold nester, taking to road verges, rooftops and airport runways. Aggressively territorial. Call consists of loud and incessant screeching, heard day or night. **CONSERVATION** Native/Not Threatened.

Juvenile

Adult

Chatham Island Snipe ■ *Coenocorypha pusilla* 20cm ⓔ

DESCRIPTION First of NZ snipes; small, rotund 'wader' with long, yellowish bill and short legs. Face and upperparts striped brown and buff; back and wings also mottled black. Belly feathers pale with less defined markings.

DISTRIBUTION Restricted to Māngere, Rangatira and Star Keys in Rēkohu/Chatham Islands. Formerly also on Chatham and Pitt Islands, where vagrants occur. **HABITS AND HABITAT** Forages for invertebrates by day and night in forest undergrowth. On moonlit nights performs mythical hakawai display: *queeyoo* calls followed by loud roar caused by tail feathers while diving at speed over the canopy, with other birds calling excitedly from the ground. Main call a husky *whew-whew-whew*. **CONSERVATION** Endemic/Nationally Vulnerable. Stable population estimated at 2,000–4,000 individuals.

Snares Island Snipe ■ *Coenocorypha huegeli* 22cm ⓔ
(tutukiwi)

DESCRIPTION Dark, stocky snipe. Light brown bill ashy towards tip; stubby legs pale yellow. Face boldly striped; brown and black mottling with buff-edged feathers overall and barring across belly. Female has greenish-grey legs. **DISTRIBUTION** Endemic to Tini Heke/The Snares group; introduced in 2005 to Putauhinu S of Rakiura/Stewart Island.

Subsequently translocated to nearby islands including Whenua Hou/Codfish Island. **HABITS AND HABITAT** Invertebrate diet gathered by probing bill into soil, in areas with dense ground cover. Also executes hakawai display (refer to text, above). **CONSERVATION** Endemic/Naturally Uncommon. Island populations threatened by accidental introduction of invasive animals such as rats. Back-up populations also established in part to fill niche of recently extinct **South Island Snipe** C. *iredalei*.

Subantarctic Snipe ■ *Coenocorypha aucklandica* 23cm (e)

DESCRIPTION ssp. *aucklandica* (Auckland Island), *meinertzhagenae* (Antipodes Island), *perseverance* (Campbell Island). Cryptically patterned brown and blackish snipe with subtle variation across its range. Feathers edged buff; belly pale and unmarked. Long bill grey-brown. Legs dull yellow, barring Antipodes birds, which have pale grey legs. **DISTRIBUTION** Found on Auckland Islands (excluding main island), Antipodes Islands and Campbell Islands, all in NZ subantarctic. **HABITS AND HABITAT** Keeps to dense vegetation of tussock, herb fields and shrubland. Typically responds to disturbance by flushing into the air with loud, whirring wingbeats. Also performs hakawai aerial display (see text, opposite). **CONSERVATION** Endemic/Naturally Uncommon.

Campbell Island subspecies   *Antipodes Island subspecies*

Ruddy Turnstone ■ *Arenaria interpres* 22–24cm

DESCRIPTION ssp. *interpres*. Stout wader with black wedge-shaped bill and short orange legs. Non-breeders have patterned brown upperparts, blackish breast and white belly. Striking chestnut, black and white when breeding. White wing-bars, scapulars and back notable in flight. Juveniles duller brown than adults. **DISTRIBUTION** Summer migrant from Arctic; third most numerous, with up to 3,000 during summer. Widespread along coast but most visit upper NI harbours. Few overwinter. Found globally.

HABITS AND HABITAT Favours estuaries and mudflats, flocking to shell banks to roost with other waders. Specialized bill to flip stones and shells in search of marine invertebrates. Main call a whistling *kew-kew-kew*. **CONSERVATION** Native/ Migrant. Loss of mudflats due to land reclamation and development in Yellow Sea is affecting food sources.

Breeding adult (left) with non-breeders

Juvenile

Breeding adult

Non-breeding adult

Bar-tailed Godwit

■ *Limosa lapponica* 39–42cm
(kuaka)

DESCRIPTION ssp. *baueri* (Eastern). Iconic long-legged wader. Most often observed in non-breeding plumage; lightly streaked grey-brown above with whitish belly, rump and brow-stripe. Wing-tips black; barred underwings and tail evident in flight. Breeding birds gain brick-red colouring below (washed out on females). Juveniles resemble non-breeding adults, except for neatly buff and brown spangled back. Legs black; two-toned pink and black bill slightly upcurved, and noticeably longer on females (also larger birds overall) than males. **DISTRIBUTION** Abundant summer migrant. Upwards of 70,000 birds spend austral summer around NZ coast. Migrates to breeding grounds in Alaskan and Siberian high Arctic via East Asian-Australasian Flyway and Yellow Sea. Many birds also overwinter, mostly juveniles. **HABITS AND HABITAT** Performs longest non-stop flight of any bird, travelling about 11,000km southwards across Pacific Ocean after breeding in little over a week. Tight-knit flocks forage actively on exposed mudflats for bivalves and crustaceans, then at high tide fly in twisting flocks to roost on adjacent shell banks, sandspits and playing fields. Gives series of calls ranging from scratchy *kew-kew-kew* to staccato, repetitive *tititi*. **CONSERVATION** Native/Declining. Research indicates annual decline of 2 per cent, driven by degradation and loss of habitat in Yellow Sea.

Black-tailed Godwit ■ *Limosa limosa* 36–40cm

DESCRIPTION ssp. *melanuroides* (Asiatic). Non-breeding plumage smoother mousy-grey than other godwits, with minimal patterning and indistinct supercilium. Long, straight bill pink with black tip; longer legs black. Upperwings dark brown with bold white stripe. Diagnostic white underwing and black border clearly visible in flight. White rump contrasts with black tail. Breeding birds have reddish head and breast, and dark barring underneath. **DISTRIBUTION** Uncommon summer migrant. Less than 10 reported annually. Breeds in Siberia and across Eurasia. **HABITS AND HABITAT** In NZ, birds frequent estuaries and brackish coastal lakes. They stay together if more than one is present; otherwise often join other wader flocks. Call a soft, repeated *kek*. **CONSERVATION** Native/Vagrant.

Non-breeding adult (left) with Bar-tailed Godwit

Hudsonian Godwit ■ *Limosa haemastica* 37–42cm

DESCRIPTION Typical godwit with smooth, grey-brown head and neck. Long, upturned bill pink, blacker towards tip. Crown dark, pale brow meets bill. Dark upperwings have narrow white bar. Bold black underwings diagnostic, seen when stretching or in flight. Rump white and tail black. Breeding adults develop rusty-red breast, and darker upperparts. **DISTRIBUTION** Rare migrant with less than five birds annually in NZ. Breeds around Hudson Bay, Canada, and Alaska. **HABITS AND HABITAT** Occurs in coastal wetlands and estuaries. Feeds inside flocks of Bar-tailed Godwits, probing for worms and crustaceans in shallow water and soft sediment. Call a sharp, rising *ke-ik*. **CONSERVATION** Native/Vagrant.

Non-breeding adult   *Non-breeding adult*

Eurasian Whimbrel ■ *Numenius phaeopus* 40–45cm

DESCRIPTION ssp. *variegatus* (Asiatic). Large wader with khaki plumage mottled dark brown. Long, downcurved bill characteristic, eye-stripe and crown dark, the latter with pale centre stripe. Base of lower mandible pink. Head and neck finely streaked, chin and belly whitish and underside strongly barred. Pale 'V' runs down back. Long legs greenish-grey.

DISTRIBUTION Summer migrant to NZ from Arctic breeding grounds. Less than 60 annually, with individuals occasionally overwintering. Most sightings occur in N NI and Farewell Spit. Other subspecies exist across Eurasia. **HABITS AND HABITAT** Occurs mainly on harbours, sandspits and estuaries. Diet typically invertebrates such as crustaceans. Call a piercing *ki-ki-ki-ki*, mostly heard in flight. **CONSERVATION** Native/Migrant.

Eastern Curlew ■ *Numenius madagascariensis* 60–66cm

DESCRIPTION Largest wader to reach NZ. Warm brown with streaked head and long neck; mottled back feathers; barred wings and tail. Throat and belly pale. Very long, downcurved bill pink at base, and eye black ringed white. Long legs greenish-grey. Female larger and longer billed (average 185mm vs. 150mm on male). **DISTRIBUTION**

Summer migrant from Siberia. Less than 10 reported annually, most often in September–April. **HABITS AND HABITAT** Strictly coastal away from breeding grounds, favouring harbours and estuaries with undisturbed roosts. Wary and difficult to approach. *Kroo-ee* call mostly heard in flight. **CONSERVATION** Native/Vagrant. Accelerating decline observed, with land reclamation at vital stopover points in Yellow Sea suspected to have major influence.

Red Knot ■ *Calidris canutus* 23–25cm

(huahou, Lesser Knot)

DESCRIPTION ssp. *rogersi, piersmai*. Plump wader; warm-grey above and pale below with variably speckled sides. Face faintly streaked with darker eye-stripe and crown. Black bill short to mid-length. Legs dark grey. White wing-bar and greyish rump evident in flight. Breeding birds brick-red on face, breast and belly, and spotted black above. Larger vagrant **Great Knot** *C. tenuirostris* longer-billed with stronger markings. **DISTRIBUTION** Spends summer in Australia and NZ (more common further N, especially in Auckland); breeds in Siberia. Other subspecies worldwide. **HABITS AND HABITAT** Long-distance migrant generally present in September–April. Favours tidal mudflats, using shell banks and sandspits to roost in enormous flocks. Diet mainly molluscs. Call a short *peep-peep*. **CONSERVATION** Native/Declining.

Non-breeding adult

Breeding adult

Red-necked Stint

■ *Calidris ruficollis* 13–16cm

DESCRIPTION Tiny wader. White below and speckled grey above with brown wash over wings and dark primaries. Breeding adults trade white for deep orange over face and upperparts. Short, tapering bill and black legs. Juveniles similar to basic adults, with richer brown tones above. **DISTRIBUTION** Locally common summer migrant; about 100 visit annually. Key sites include Manukau Harbour, Auckland, Lake Ellesmere, Canterbury, and Awarua Bay, Southland. **HABITS AND HABITAT** Fossicks for small invertebrates on coastal mudflats and saltmarshes. Departs March–April and utilizes East Asian-Australasian Flyway to reach breeding grounds in high Arctic. Fairly silent in NZ but will give bubbly murmur. **CONSERVATION** Native/Migrant.

Non-breeding adult

Breeding adult

Sanderling ■ *Calidris alba* 18–20cm

DESCRIPTION Small, active shorebird nearly always encountered in non-breeding plumage. White below and pale grey above; distinctive dark upperwings with white flash

running along them. Rump white with greyish centre, tail grey. Stout, straight bill and short legs black. Breeding plumage adults bronze above speckled black. Juveniles similar to basic adults, but boldly marked black and white above. **DISTRIBUTION** Rare summer migrant, with less than three birds annually reaching NZ. Most often visits Kaipara Harbour, Farewell Spit and Awarua Bay in Southland. Cosmopolitan. **HABITS AND HABITAT** Coastal, preferring surf beaches and sandy inlets. Runs speedily along the water's edge in avoidance of incoming tide. Main call a chirpy *kwit*. **CONSERVATION** Native/Vagrant.

Non-breeding adult

Curlew Sandpiper ■ *Calidris ferruginea* 18–23cm

DESCRIPTION Small wader, in non-breeding plumage mottled warm grey above and dirty white below. Black eye sits under prominent white supercilium. Long black bill fine and downcurved, and long legs dark. White rump and underwing seen in flight. Breeding

plumage birds gain rusty-red colouring on head and breast, with orange and black markings across back. **DISTRIBUTION** Uncommon summer migrant; fewer than 10 birds annually (and decreasing). Most frequently seen on Manukau Harbour in Auckland and Lake Ellesmere in Canterbury. **HABITS AND HABITAT** Tends to associate with flocks of Wrybill (p. 45) while at high-tide roosts. Feeds on crustaceans, molluscs and worms from harbours and estuaries. Call a soft *chirrup*. **CONSERVATION** Native/Vagrant.

Non-breeding adult

Sharp-tailed Sandpiper ■ *Calidris acuminate* 17–22cm
(kohutapu)

DESCRIPTION Small, elegant wader. Crown chestnut, neck and breast streaked brown, and back feathers dark brown with pale fringes. White underside and eye-ring, and indistinct brow-stripe. In breeding plumage adults develop orange wash over breast and back, with bold black chevrons across body. Short, straight bill black with brown base, and legs yellow. **DISTRIBUTION** Less than 30 birds reach NZ annually during summer from breeding grounds in N Siberia. **HABITS AND HABITAT** Forages on tidal mudflats and occasionally along freshwater lakes. Omnivorous. Call a sharp *peep-peep*. **CONSERVATION** Native/Migrant. Marked decline in recent years probably due to development in Yellow Sea; 100–200 were seen each year until 1990s.

Non-breeding adult

Pectoral Sandpiper ■ *Calidris melanotos* 19–24cm

DESCRIPTION Bulky wader with drooping, brown to black bill. Flecked head with pale eye-ring, throat and brow; intense dark streaking down to breast with sharp margin before white belly. Legs and bill-base yellow. Male up to 50 per cent heavier than female. **DISTRIBUTION** Rare summer migrant; less than 10 birds reach NZ annually, as far as Chatham Islands. Breeds in Arctic Circle from Siberia to North America. **HABITS AND HABITAT** Found on mudflats in harbours and estuaries, and verges of lowland lakes. Fairly silent during austral summer; will give a short trill. **CONSERVATION** Native/Vagrant. In 2016, a Cox's Sandpiper (hybrid Pectoral x Curlew Sandpiper) was seen at Lake Ellesmere.

Non-breeding adult

Terek Sandpiper ■ *Xenus cinereus* 22–25cm

DESCRIPTION Small, plump wader; 'kind-faced' with stripe through eye. Plumage pale grey-brown with white underparts, and dark grey upperwings with white trailing edges. Bright orange legs and long, upturned bill with orange base distinctive. Breeding birds similar but more boldly marked, with darker bill. **DISTRIBUTION** Up to three birds visit

NZ in most years. Breeds in N Russia; widespread from Africa to Australasia. **HABITS AND HABITAT** Specialist of mudflats, sandspits and estuaries. Forages by pecking and probing at the surface. Runs rapidly with head down if disturbed or if it notices prey from afar. Call 3–4 short, descending whistles. **CONSERVATION** Native/ Vagrant. Increasingly rare visitor.

Marsh Sandpiper ■ *Tringa stagnatilis* 22–25cm

DESCRIPTION Slender wader with thin, straight bill and long yellow-green legs. Whitish plumage overall, apart from grey upperwings, face and crown. Dark wings against white back and tail distinctive in flight. Breeding birds gain black speckling over grey upperparts. **DISTRIBUTION** Summer migrant; less than five birds recorded annually. Breeds across C Asia. **HABITS AND HABITAT** Rarely far from coast, but favours shallow lakes or brackish ponds over tidal mudflats. Individuals can remain for years at a time. Call a high-pitched *pew*. **CONSERVATION** Native/Vagrant. Intensive agriculture around northern breeding grounds has led to decline in range.

Breeding adult

Wandering Tattler ■ *Tringa incana* 26–30cm

DESCRIPTION Slate-grey shorebird with thick, straight bill and yellow legs. Diffuse pale belly, and brow that meets dark eye, which has narrow white ring. Wing, crown and lores darker grey. In rarely encountered breeding plumage, face and underparts whiten and develop dark chevron patterns. **DISTRIBUTION** Up to three birds visit NZ in most years. Breeds in Arctic N America, ranging throughout Americas and Pacific during austral summer. **HABITS AND HABITAT** Most often encountered on rocky shores and exposed coasts, but also uses sandspits and mudflats, where it hunts for worms and crustaceans. Calls consist of varied repeated piping sounds. **CONSERVATION** Native/Vagrant.

Non-breeding adult

Grey-tailed Tattler ■ *Tringa brevipes* 25cm

DESCRIPTION Grey shorebird. Non-breeding adults feature dark loral stripe in contrast with bold white supercilium, as well as white throat and belly. White underside more extensive in alternate plumage, with fine dark barring over breast and flanks. Stout bill black, sometimes with dull yellow base; legs bright yellow. Best distinguished from Wandering Tattler (above) by lighter plumage and brow, and 2-syllable call.

DISTRIBUTION Rare summer migrant; about five individuals reported annually, breeding in Siberia. **HABITS AND HABITAT** Occurs mainly on harbours and estuaries, and less often on shore platforms and sandy beaches. Long-distance migrant along East Asian-Australasian Flyway. Call a repetitive, rising *too-eep*. **CONSERVATION** Native/Vagrant.

Non-breeding adult

Brown Skua ▪ *Stercorarius antarcticus* 52–64cm; WS 126–160cm
(hākoakoa, Southern Skua)

DESCRIPTION ssp. *lonnbergi* (Subantarctic). Heavy dark brown seabird; adults weigh 1.5–2.2kg. Hooked bill; eyes and legs black. Long, broad wings have white patch across base of primaries. Sexes alike, but female much larger than male. **DISTRIBUTION** Breeds on islets off Rakiura/Stewart Island, around Rēkohu/Chatham Islands and subantarctic islands. Sometimes encountered at sea around mainland NZ. Occurs throughout Southern Ocean. **HABITS AND HABITAT** Stays near coast while breeding, and normally spends winter

at sea. Opportunistic feeder, harassing other seabirds for their catch and going as far as to prey on smaller penguins and petrels. Territorial display 'Viking helmet' involves wing raising accompanied by gull-like *ah-ah-ah* call. **CONSERVATION** Native/Nationally Vulnerable.

South Polar Skua ▪ *Stercorarius maccormicki* 50–55cm; WS 130–140cm

DESCRIPTION Bulky skua with plumage ranging from blond to dark brown and large white flashes on wings. Pale morph has contrasting dark wings, as does grey-brown intermediate morph. Dark morph similar to the larger Brown Skua (above) but with

smaller bill and plainer back. Juveniles greyer and plainer than adults. **DISTRIBUTION** Regular but rare migrant through deep waters around NZ in spring and autumn. Breeds along coast of Antarctica, moving to northern hemisphere in March–October. **HABITS AND HABITAT** Less piratic than other skuas, but will attack penguin eggs and chicks near breeding grounds. Territorial and monogamous, with both parents sharing nesting duties. Harsh call often given with wings raised, as well as quacks and screams in colony. **CONSERVATION** Native/Migrant.

Pomarine Skua ■ *Stercorarius pomarinus* 65–78cm; WS 110–138cm
(Pomarine Jaeger)

DESCRIPTION Robust, barrel-chested seabird with heavy hooked bill and variable plumage; take care to separate from more common Arctic Skua (below). Pale phase in basic plumage has whitish face and belly, and messy sooty-brown feathering on head, collar and back. Broad wings dark apart from white flash on underwing. Dark phase entirely dark brown. Breeding birds develop sharper plumage and long, spoon-shaped tail streamers. Juveniles barred underneath. **DISTRIBUTION** Rare but regular summer migrant seen coastally or at sea around mainland NZ. Cosmopolitan, breeding in Arctic Circle. **HABITS AND HABITAT** Pelagic practitioner of piracy, harassing gulls, terns and even gannets for their catches; also catches fish and scavenges when necessary. Gives piercing *kipp*ing and *mew* calls. **CONSERVATION** Native/Migrant.

Non-breeding adult

Arctic Skua ■ *Stercorarius parasiticus* 46–67cm; WS 107–125cm
(Parasitic Jaeger)

DESCRIPTION Sleek, hook-billed seabird with many plumages. Most common is dark morph; entirely blackish-brown, sometimes with pale nape. Pale morph has buff face and dark cap, brown collar and back, and white belly. Intermediate morph in between. All have dark, pointed tail and wings with white flash underneath. Breeding birds neater, with long tail streamers. Immatures have mottled underside. Active and graceful flight with many twists and turns.

Daintier **Long-tailed Skua** *S. longicaudus* a much rarer visitor. **DISTRIBUTION** Common coastal Arctic migrant to NZ during Sep–Mar. **HABITS AND HABITAT** Occurs inshore around estuaries, harbours and beaches. Regularly accompanies gull and tern flocks as a kleptoparasite, pursuing and robbing them of their meals. **CONSERVATION** Native/Migrant.

Non-breeding adult dark morph   *Non-breeding adult pale morph*

Adult

Juvenile

Southern Black-backed Gull

■ *Larus dominicanus* 49–62cm; WS 106–142cm
(karoro, Kelp Gull)

DESCRIPTION ssp. *dominicanus*. Large, bulky gull with white head, body and tail. Back and upperwings dusky black, latter bordered in white. Eyelid orange, iris pale. Strong bill yellow with red spot near tip. Legs pale green to yellow. Juveniles mottled black and brown with black bills and legs, developing adult plumage over three years. **DISTRIBUTION** Abundant over mainland NZ and most outlying islands. Throughout S hemisphere. **HABITS AND HABITAT** Coast, inland lakes and riverbeds, urban areas and farmland. Breeds in colonies sometimes exceeding 1,000 pairs, utilizing untidy piles of twigs and grass as nests. Opportunistic feeder on fish to food scraps. Call a loud, persistent *e-ha*. **CONSERVATION** Native/Not Threatened.

Red-billed Gull ■ *Chroicocephalus novaehollandiae* 36–44cm; WS 91–96cm
(tarāpunga, Silver Gull)

DESCRIPTION ssp. *scopulinus*. Familiar small gull. Adults white overall with silvery wings and black and white wing-tips. Stout bill, eye-ring and legs vivid red in summer, dark red in winter. Iris pale. Bill and iris of juveniles black, with dirty brown speckling across back. **DISTRIBUTION** Mostly coastal resident across NZ, from Three Kings Islands S to Rakiura/Stewart Island, as well as Chatham Islands and some subantarctic islands. Breeds inland at Lake Rotorua. Also across Australia and New Caledonia. **HABITS AND HABITAT** Frequents beaches, estuaries, rocky shores, urban parks and commercial areas, taking food scraps; preference for fish and chips. Natural diet small fish and invertebrates. Call a typically raucous *ahwrr*. **CONSERVATION** Native/Declining.

Breeding adult

Juvenile

Black-billed Gull ■ *Chroicocephalus bulleri* 35–38cm; WS 81–96cm ⓔ
(tarāpuka, Buller's Gull)

DESCRIPTION Easily confused with the Red-billed Gull (opposite). Adults of this more elegant gull have lighter pearl-grey wings and less black on the tips. Longer, more slender bill and wings are the key way to identify this species, not bill colour, which can actually be red in non-breeding birds. Eye-ring and legs also black in breeding birds, transforming to deep crimson afterwards. Iris pale. Immature birds have pinkish legs and bill, the latter black at tip. Trailing edges of upperwings have dark markings. Juveniles have black iris (lightens with age) and brown speckling across back. **DISTRIBUTION** Spans from large harbours of upper NI, inland to Lake Taupo, down to Manuwatu and Wellington. Common throughout SI and Rakiura/Stewart Island. **HABITS AND HABITAT** Dense colonies breed on shell banks and braided riverbeds, feeding along nearby streams, estuaries and pasture. Diet of small fish, crustaceans and invertebrates. Large colonies can change position from year to year. Most SI breeders migrate to coast after their chicks fledge in summer, and can be seen out to sea. Call a grating *ahwrr*, deeper than that of Red-billed. **CONSERVATION** Endemic/Declining. Disturbance and predation by both mammalian predators and birds such as Southern Black-backed Gull (opposite) at nesting sites, generally of eggs and chicks.

Breeding adult

Juvenile

Non-breeding adult

Adults on nests

Black Noddy ■ *Anous minutus*
35–37cm; WS 66–72cm

DESCRIPTION ssp. *minutus*. Elegant matte-black tern with white crown that grades into nape. Long, pointed bill and webbed feet black. Lores and iris jet-black with partial white eye-ring. Tapered wings crescent shaped, and tail lightly forked. **DISTRIBUTION** Breeds locally on Kermadec Islands; straggles to mainland NZ. Elsewhere in Pacific and Atlantic Oceans. **HABITS AND HABITAT** The name 'noddy' may originate from head-dipping displays typical of the genus. Flocks forage for fish and squid, and also pirate food from other seabirds. Nests on cliffs, in caves, in trees or on the ground. Call a rattling croak. **CONSERVATION** Native/Nationally Vulnerable.

Brown Noddy ■ *Anous stolidus* 40–45cm; WS 75–86cm

DESCRIPTION Sleek brown tern with long, dark wings and tail. Black mask, partial eye-ring and silver cap distinctive. Juveniles slightly darker than adults, with reduced pale crown. Most similar to the Black Noddy (above), which is smaller and blacker with white cap. **DISTRIBUTION** Local to Kermadec Islands in NZ, where it is known to nest

on Curtis Island, but also occurs throughout tropics worldwide. **HABITS AND HABITAT** Gregarious while feeding at sea, skimming the water for small fish. Generally colonial, nesting on cliffs, trees or bushes. Single egg in clutch hatches after about 35 days. Many harsh rattling and grating calls given. **CONSERVATION** Native/Coloniser. In NZ, 25 pairs estimated when colony discovered in 1989; probably now well established.

Grey Noddy ■ *Anous albivittus* 25–30cm; 46–61cm
(Grey Ternlet)

DESCRIPTION Dainty noddy with silvery plumage and mid-grey across wings and tail. Flight feathers slate-grey. Black bill long and tapered; iris dark with black patch in front and white behind. Long legs and feet black except for orange webs. **DISTRIBUTION** Breeds across Kermadec Islands NE of mainland NZ, with small flocks visiting Mokohinau Islands in Hauraki Gulf, Sugarloaf Rock in Poor Knights Islands and Three Kings Islands during summer. Occurs throughout tropical Pacific. **HABITS AND HABITAT** Roosts on sheer cliffs in loose flocks, feeding in the ocean on tiny fish, squid and krill. Courtship display performed hovering and weaving in the wind. Call a gravelly *craw*. **CONSERVATION** Native/ Naturally Uncommon.

White Noddy ■ *Gygis alba* 25–31cm; WS 76–87cm
(White Tern)

DESCRIPTION ssp. *candida*. Slender all-white bird with narrow, pointed wings and forked tail. Wedge-shaped bill bluish-black, and black eye hidden in black mask. Legs bluish-grey with yellow webs. Juveniles faintly marked brown above. **DISTRIBUTION** Occurs worldwide throughout tropics and subtropics, but in NZ waters nests only on Raoul of the Kermadec Islands. **HABITS AND HABITAT** Unusual nesting technique; lays a single egg on a bare branch or fork of a tree. Fish and squid are taken from the ocean's surface. Call a repetitive, raspy *ew-erk*. **CONSERVATION** Native/Nationally Critical. Perhaps only 10 pairs in NZ, but hundreds of thousands globally.

Juvenile

Sooty Tern ▪ *Onychoprion fuscatus*
33–36cm; WS 82–94cm

DESCRIPTION ssp. *serratus*. Striking tern dark brown above with forked tail. Crown and eye-stripe black; forehead, leading edge of wing and underside clean white. Juveniles entirely dark brown with pale spotting on wings and rump. **DISTRIBUTION** Common globally throughout tropics. Large numbers breed on Kermadec Islands NE of NZ, rarely reaching mainland. **HABITS AND HABITAT** Nests in dense, noisy colonies on rock stacks, islands and atolls. Fledglings spend three years at sea before returning to breed, and can live for more than 30 years. Main call heard at colonies a cat-like *werk*. **CONSERVATION** Native/Recovering since mammalian predators eradicated from Raoul Island in 2004.

Adult

Little Tern ▪ *Sternula albifrons* 22–28cm; WS 45–55cm
(tara teo)

DESCRIPTION ssp. *sinensis* (Eastern). Tiny white tern. Breeding birds have yellow-orange legs and matching long bill with black tip. Crown, lores and eye-stripe black. Pearl-grey wings and back, with dark outer primaries. Crown of non-breeders recedes back to nape around to eye, and bill turns completely dark. Immatures alike with dark carpal bar. **DISTRIBUTION** Coastal around NI and SI, usually settling further N. Breeds across Australia to E Asia as far as Sri Lanka. **HABITS AND HABITAT** Up to 100 birds migrate to harbours and estuaries in NZ for summer, rarely overwintering. When roosting, flocks take to shell banks and mudflats, often alongside shorebirds. Call a harsh *kyip*. **CONSERVATION** Native/Migrant.

Breeding adult

Non-breeding adult

Fairy Tern ■ *Sternula nereis* 22–27cm; WS 44–53cm
(tara iti)

DESCRIPTION ssp. *davisae* (New Zealand). Considered NZ's rarest bird. Tiny, delicate tern with bright yellow bill and legs. Forehead white; crown black continuing to just in front of black eye. Plumage white below and pearly-grey on wings and back. Crown of non-breeders recedes back to nape, and bill gains dark tip. Legs and bill of juveniles black.

Immature

DISTRIBUTION Relict population nests only on eastern Northland coastline at Waipu, Mangawhai, Te Arai and Pakiri Beaches. Winters on Kaipara Harbour to W, occasionally also breeding at Papakanui Spit. Two other subspecies in Australia and New Caledonia, which could be distinct species. **HABITS AND HABITAT** Nests primarily on sand dunes in Oct–Mar, laying 1–2 eggs in small scrape. Pairs re-lay several times if nest fails. Favours small fish including gobies and sole, which it forages from nearby sheltered inlets and estuaries. Main call a rising *kirikip*. **CONSERVATION** Native/ Nationally Critical, with fewer than 40 remaining in NZ. Impacted by human disturbance due to preference for white-sand beaches, storm events washing away nests, low genetic diversity affecting chick output and mammalian predation. Gargantuan amounts of resources and effort are dedicated towards protecting them.

Non-breeding adult

Breeding adult

White-winged Black Tern
■ *Chlidonias leucopterus* 20–23cm; WS 60–67cm

DESCRIPTION Small tern unmistakable in breeding plumage; completely black with back and bright white wings and tail. Non-breeding birds encountered more often: white underparts and head, except for dark 'earmuff' markings. Long wings dusky-grey with black primaries. Slender bill black, and legs dark red. **DISTRIBUTION** Rare but regular migrant to NI and SI. Up to 20 annually. Four NZ nesting records; also occurs across Eurasia, Africa and Australia. **HABITS AND HABITAT** Found around lagoons, rivers and lakes. Hawks for insects over water's surface. Calls high-pitched purrs and squeaks. **CONSERVATION** Native/Migrant.

Immature

Breeding adult

Black-fronted Tern ■ *Chlidonias albostriatus* 28–30cm; WS 65–72cm (e)
(tarapirohe)

DESCRIPTION Slender tern with bright orange bill and legs. Breeding birds feature neat black cap with white stripe under eye and silvery-grey plumage overall. Pointed wings and tail distinctive. Non-breeders have receded black caps; juveniles have dark bills and mottled brown plumage. **DISTRIBUTION** Breeds exclusively in E SI from Marlborough to Southland. Wintering birds travel to coast, as far N as Bay of Plenty, rarely further. **HABITS AND HABITAT** Braided riverbed specialist. Frequently seen hawking for flying insects over fields, rivers or at sea. Calls are high-pitched purrs and squeaks. **CONSERVATION** Endemic/Nationally Endangered. Heavily impacted by mammalian predators, especially cats and mustelids.

Breeding adult

Juvenile

Antarctic Tern ■ *Sterna vittata* 31–38cm; WS 72–79cm

DESCRIPTION ssp. *bethunei* (New Zealand). Stocky, medium-sized tern, gaining breeding plumage during austral summer. Black cap meets base of deep red bill. Plumage mid-grey overall, except white cheeks, rump and forked tail. Pointed wings greyish-black at tips. Non-breeding plumage similar but with reduced crown, white underparts and somewhat duller bill. Immatures have black bills; juveniles initially patterned buff and black.

DISTRIBUTION Breeds on all NZ subantarctic islands and certain islands around Rakiura/Stewart Island. Other subspecies range throughout Southern Ocean. **HABITS AND HABITAT** Relatively sedentary, nesting in lightly vegetated or exposed rocky areas. Catches small fish via contact dipping and plunge diving. Call a rattling *keh-keh*. **CONSERVATION** Native/Nationally Increasing.

Immature

Breeding adult

Arctic Tern ■ *Sterna paradisaea* 33–35cm; WS 66–72cm

DESCRIPTION Elegant tern, in breeding plumage during austral winter. Black cap continues to deep red bill; plumage pale grey overall with white cheeks, rump and forked tail. Wings broad; with defined black trailing edge near tips. Reddish legs very short. Non-breeders lose colour in bill, and cap is reduced to black band behind head with speckled crown. Immatures have dark scalloping over back. Take care in ID. **DISTRIBUTION** Rare Arctic migrant, can be seen passing through at sea around NZ, and occasionally on coast. **HABITS AND HABITAT** Sometimes intermingles with flocks of White-fronted Terns (p. 70) roosting on beaches or rocks. Rarely vocal on migration, main call a *kree-ah*. **CONSERVATION** Native/Migrant.

Non-breeding adult

Breeding adult

White-fronted Tern ■ *Sterna striata* 35–43cm; WS 79–82cm
(tara)

DESCRIPTION Medium-sized tern with fine black bill. Breeding-plumage birds have smart black crown that starts from nape but does not meet bill, creating white front. Overall white on neck, rump and underparts, going into pale grey on wings and back, and dark leading edge on primaries. Long outer-tail feathers characteristic. Eye dark, and legs maroon to black. In basic plumage black crown recedes to behind head, with several dark flecks remaining. The vagrant Common Tern (opposite) is smaller, slightly greyer above with a dark carpal bar. Sexes alike, and juvenile plumage similar to basic, with brown mottling on back and shoulders. **DISTRIBUTION** Common along coast from Northland southwards to Rakiura/Stewart Island, as well as Chatham and Auckland Islands. Some birds migrate to S Australia, where small numbers also breed. **HABITS AND HABITAT**

Breeds in colonies on sand dunes, shell banks, riverbeds and rock faces, where 1–2 eggs are laid in small scrape. Location can change from year to year based on food availability or disturbance. Birds feed at sea, in estuaries or harbours where they catch small fish, diving from height of 5–10m. Gives a *krrrp* type call often and a zappy *kek* in flight. **CONSERVATION** Native/Declining. At risk from predation and colony disturbance by storms events and humans.

Juvenile

Breeding pair

Common Tern ■ *Sterna hirundo* 32–36cm; WS 72–82cm

DESCRIPTION ssp. *longipennis* (Eastern). Slender typical tern, take care with ID. Breeding plumage grey, with face and black cap that meets narrow black bill. Long wings grey with darker leading edge. Cap is reduced and primaries blacken in non-breeders. Immatures similar with browner cap. **DISTRIBUTION** Despite name, rare but annual visitor to NI and SI. Breeds throughout N hemisphere. **HABITS AND HABITAT** Found at sea, on beaches and in estuaries. Often associates with larger White-fronted Terns (opposite). Call a high-pitched, gravelly *kerrr*. **CONSERVATION** Native/Vagrant.

Breeding adult

Immature

Australian Tern ■ *Gelochelidon macrotarsa* 35–42cm; WS 100–115cm

DESCRIPTION Bulky tern with heavy black bill, split from smaller N Hemisphere breeding Gull-billed Tern. Underparts white; wings pale grey with dark outer primaries. Breeding birds have neat black cap from bill to nape. Legs long and black. Non-breeding and immature birds slightly darker on back, as well as white on head except for dark patch around eye and cheek. **DISTRIBUTION** Fewer than 5 in NZ at any time, from Australia. Invasions of up to 20 have occurred. Most records from Tasman, Lake Ellesmere and Southland, with first nesting recorded for NZ at Awarua Bay in 2019. **HABITS AND HABITAT** Occurs around harbours and sheltered river mouths. Occasionally visits freshwater lakes. Call a raucous *wu-erk*. **CONSERVATION** Native/Colonizer.

Breeding adult

Caspian Tern ▪ *Hydroprogne caspia* 47–54cm; WS 130–145cm
(taranui)

DESCRIPTION Largest tern species. Distinctive thick red bill, black at tip. Mainly white plumage with pale grey upperwings and dark outer primaries. Short, forked tail. Neat black cap meets bill on breeding birds, with subtle crest on nape. Non-breeding birds trade their black cap for fine grey streaking on crown and dark patch around eye. Immature birds similar, but have duller orange bill, and juveniles have mottled backs. Iris and short legs black. **DISTRIBUTION** Widespread throughout mainland NZ in modest numbers. Elsewhere scattered across N America, Africa, Eurasia and Australia. **HABITS**

Juvenile

AND HABITAT Frequents coastlines, harbours, estuaries, rivers and lakes; less common inland and at sea. Colony nester, but outside of breeding often seen singly or in pairs. Feeds almost entirely on fish caught by plunge diving. Call a gravelly *ark-ark*. **CONSERVATION** Native/ Nationally Vulnerable. Around 1,400 pairs may nest in NZ. Colonies prone to desertion if disturbed.

Breeding adult

Red-tailed Tropicbird ■ *Phaethon rubricauda* 95–105cm; WS 110–120cm
(amokura)

DESCRIPTION Pure white seabird with heavy red bill. Black patch sits just in front of large dark eye. Crimson tail streamers grow to average of 35cm, and black feet visible when in flight. Dark-billed juveniles barred black across crown, nape and upperwings, and lack streamers. Rare vagrant **White-tailed Tropicbirds** *P. lepturus* have yellow bills. **DISTRIBUTION** Breeds on Kermadec Islands and strays to seas off Northland in summers; very rare further S. Elsewhere, breeds on tropical islands throughout Pacific and Indian Oceans. **HABITS AND HABITAT** High-flying pelagic species with entirely piscivorous diet. Call a rough, repeated *kraw*. **CONSERVATION** Native/Nationally Increasing.

Adult

Australian Pelican ■ *Pelecanus conspicullatus* 152–188cm; WS 230–260cm
(perikana)

DESCRIPTION Huge, long-necked bird; white with broad black wings, rump and tail. Small crest on nape also flecked with grey. Eye dark with yellow orbital ring. Enormous pink bill and throat-pouch the largest of any bird. Breeding birds have stunning blue and red colouring on bill, with yellow tip. Short legs slate-grey. Immatures duller than adults. **DISTRIBUTION** Rare visitor to NZ from Australia. Invasions can occur; at least 15 reached the Kaipara Harbour in Northland in 2012. **HABITS AND HABITAT** Occurs on large expanses of open water, including lakes, wetlands, harbours and estuaries. Movement dependent on food availability (fish, crustaceans and insects). Call a low, guttural growl. **CONSERVATION** Native/Vagrant.

Adults

Eastern Rockhopper Penguin ■ *Eudyptes filholi* 45–55cm
(tawaki piki toka)

DESCRIPTION Crested penguin; black with glossy white front and massive orange-brown bill. Slender yellow supercilium goes across face, flaring outwards in crest. Feet and

bare skin around bill pale pink. **DISTRIBUTION** NZ populations on Campbell, Auckland and Antipodes Islands, as well as Macquarie Island. Elsewhere in S Indian Ocean. **HABITS AND HABITAT** Birds return to land only to breed during spring and moult, otherwise spending months at sea travelling thousands of kilometres. Breeding adults make loud, braying calls often accompanied by ritualized displays. **CONSERVATION** Native/ Nationally Vulnerable. Large-scale decline in 1900s thought to be from low food availability attributed to climate change.

Adult

Adult

Fiordland Crested Penguin
■ *Eudyptes pachyrynchus* 55–60cm ⓔ
(tawaki)

DESCRIPTION Stout black and white penguin with yellow crest extending from above chunky orange bill down behind head. Face black, with white streaking just below dark red eye. **DISTRIBUTION** Endemic to SI from S West Coast down to Fiordland, Rakiura/Stewart Island and surrounding islands. Vagrants occur as far N as Northland and W to Australia. **HABITS AND HABITAT** Breeds in loose, scattered colonies of 20–200 breeding pairs. Location ranges from native forest to sea caves and boulder beaches. Before moult, birds undertake a marathon swim halfway to Antarctica and back in just two months. Call an ascending rattle, combined with yelps and hisses. **CONSERVATION** Endemic/Declining.

Snares Crested Penguin ■ *Eudyptes robustus* 60cm e
(pokotiwha)

DESCRIPTION Typical penguin with
black upperparts and white underparts.
Yellow crest extends from above nasal
groove past red eye. Large orange bill set
apart from face by pink gape. Feet pink
with dark nails and soles. Juveniles smaller
than adults, with dark blue plumage and
blackish bill. **DISTRIBUTION** Endemic
to Tini Heke/The Snares. Rare visitor
to mainland and other subantarctic
islands. **HABITS AND HABITAT** Nests
in crowded colonies of to 1,000 pairs,
which can be located inland as well as
on shore. Forages in SW Tasman Sea
outside breeding season. Diet of various
cephalopods, crustaceans and fish.
Noisy; gives a squawking *kruk* and deep,
trumpeting *honk* at sea. **CONSERVATION**
Endemic/Naturally Uncommon.

Adults

Erect-crested Penguin ■ *Eudyptes sclateri* 65–67cm e
(tawaki nana hī)

DESCRIPTION Heaviest of NZ's crested
penguins. Black above and white below.
Yellow crest very broad; begins near gape
extending off behind crown. Pink facial skin
borders heavy, dark orange bill; iris deep
red. Immatures have less extensive crests
and paler throats. **DISTRIBUTION** Breeds
exclusively on subantarctic Antipodes and
Bounty Islands. Moulting individuals show up
occasionally along SI coastline in late summer.
HABITS AND HABITAT Breeds in small
colonies in native forest bordering isolated
bays and headlands. Around March post-
moult departs to sea, not returning to colony
until mid-winter. Diet consists of various
cephalopods, crustaceans and fish. Typical
penguin squawk, deeper than that of relatives.
CONSERVATION Endemic/Declining.

Adult

Yellow-eyed Penguin ■ *Megadyptes antipodes* 65–78cm ⓔ
(hoiho)

DESCRIPTION Tall, robust penguin with characteristic pale yellow band around back of head encompassing both eyes. Iris yellow, eye-ring and gape pink, in line with long, red-tipped bill. Head otherwise light brown with yellow and black streaking over face and crown. Underparts white; back, tail and outsides of flippers slate-grey. Feet pink with black soles. Sexes alike; male larger than female. Juveniles lack yellow band and have greyer overall head. **DISTRIBUTION** Northern population in lower SI around Banks

Peninsula in Canterbury, and along Otago coast from Oamaru down to Catlins in Southland. Key sites include Kaitiki Point and Otago Peninsula. Also on Rakiura/Stewart Island and adjacent islands. Southern population in subantarctic on Auckland and Campbell Islands. **HABITS AND HABITAT** Nests in coastal scrub and forest under concealing vegetation. Dives typically 200 times a day to depths averaging 30–60m in search of small fish and squid, but capable of diving up to 150m. Main call, though infrequently heard, a piercing bray. **CONSERVATION** Endemic/Nationally Endangered. Fewer than 3,000 thought to remain, with ongoing decline attributed to predation by introduced mammals, diseases, fisheries bycatch and climate change. Also affected by human disturbance; keep at least 50m from wild birds. Being highly sensitive to variation in the ocean, can provide insight into health of marine ecosystems.

Immature

Adult

Little Penguin ▪ *Eudyptula minor* 30–33cm
(kororā, Blue Penguin)

DESCRIPTION ssp. *minor* (New Zealand), *novaehollandiae* (Australian). Smallest penguin species. Dumpy bird with bluish upperparts and glossy white underparts from chin to belly. Flippers predominately dark blue with white trailing edge (Canterbury birds also have white leading edge). Feathers on head darker around eye; cheeks pale. Heavy bill black and iris grey. Pink feet with black nails and soles. Male slightly larger than female, with more robust bill. Recently fledged young bright blue dorsally, and smaller than adults. Chicks have black downy covering and dark eyes. **DISTRIBUTION** All around coastline and surrounding offshore islands of NI, SI, Rakiura/ Stewart Island and Rēkohu/Chatham Islands. Other subspecies found along S coast of Australia, and interestingly also replaces the local form along the Otago coast, although they appear identical. **HABITS AND HABITAT** Burrows can be located in rocky crevices and banks within several hundred metres of shore. Returns to nesting areas at dusk, congregating in small groups, or 'rafts', offshore, which arrive together each night. Must stay ashore continuously for about two weeks during annual moult in Jan–Mar when all feathers are replaced simultaneously. Forages to 20km offshore, diving in pursuit of small fish, squid and crustaceans. Call comprises guttural moans and screeches. **CONSERVATION** Native/Declining. Biggest threats are mammalian predators such as cats and dogs. Starvation in years of food shortages and being hit by vehicles also contribute.

Adult

Adult

Juvenile

Snowy Albatross

■ *Diomedea exulans* 107–135cm; WS 254–350cm

(Wandering Albatross)

DESCRIPTION Largest albatross. Adults white with long, pink, tube-nosed bills and beady black eyes. Many have salmon-coloured stain on neck. Juveniles chocolate-brown apart from face and underwings. Black tail and upperwings become patchier and paler with age. Apart from palest, nearly fully white adults, very difficult to distinguish from the Antipodean Albatross (below), but noticeably larger and heavier, with huge, deep-based bill. **DISTRIBUTION** Regular but uncommon migrant to deep waters around NZ. Closest colony on Macquarie Island (Australia) in subantarctic. Widespread throughout Southern Ocean. **HABITS AND HABITAT** Pairs nest every two years in grassland. One large egg laid in December, hatching in March. Chick fledges after 7–9 months. **CONSERVATION** Native/Migrant.

Antipodean Albatross

■ *Diomedea antipodensis* 110–118cm; WS 280–330cm (e)

(toroa, New Zealand Wandering Albatross)

DESCRIPTION ssp. *antipodensis, gibsoni* (Gibson's). Large, majestic albatross with variable plumage depending on age, sex and subspecies. All feature large pink bill, dark wings and plumage that whitens with age. Adult Gibson's palest; some have peach neck stain and light brown cap. Adult Antipodeans always have dark brown cap. Juveniles chocolate-brown (white face and underwings). **DISTRIBUTION** Majority breed on Antipodes and Auckland Islands. Not uncommon in deeper waters off NZ. **HABITS AND HABITAT** Remote, windy nest sites allow for easy take-off. Cephalopods preferred but also take fish and discards from boats. Courting birds perform elaborate displays, with shrieks, roars and bill clapping. **CONSERVATION** Endemic/Nationally Critical. Rapid decline since 2004 linked to fisheries bycatch.

Gibson subspecies

Antipodean subspecies

Southern Royal Albatross

■ *Diomedea epomophora* 112–124cm; WS 290–350cm ⓔ
(toroa)

DESCRIPTION Largest albatross; pure white apart from black flight feathers and upperwings that whiten from leading edge with age. Heavy bill pale pink with black cutting edge. Juveniles have black flecks on mantle and tip to tail. **DISTRIBUTION** Majority breed on subantarctic Campbell Islands, with smaller numbers on Auckland Islands. Foraging focused around S NZ, Chile and Argentina. **HABITS AND HABITAT** Nests at 180–350m among tussock grassland and mega-herb fields; completely pelagic otherwise. Non-breeding birds and juveniles cross Southern Ocean to forage in South American waters before returning to NZ by circumnavigating the globe. Lives up to 60 years. **CONSERVATION** Endemic/ Nationally Vulnerable.

Adult

Northern Royal Albatross

■ *Diomedea sanfordi* 115–120cm; WS 270–305cm ⓔ
(toroa)

DESCRIPTION Distinguished from larger Southern Royal Albatross (above) by black leading edge to wings and more uniformly matte-black upperwings. Otherwise more or less identical, owing to white body and mantle, and large, hooked pink bill with black cutting edge. Females occasionally have dark speckling on crown, and juveniles on back. **DISTRIBUTION** Breeds on three islets in Chatham Archipelago, as well as Taiaroa Head on Otago Peninsula, unique in being the only mainland albatross colony. Forages off S America. **HABITS AND HABITAT** Juvenile birds return to colonies when 3–4 years old, and usually breed at eight years. Colony call a bloodcurdling scream interspersed with whines and bill clapping. **CONSERVATION** Endemic/Nationally Vulnerable.

Adult

Black-browed Albatross

■ *Thalassarche melanophris* 80–96cm; WS 210–250cm
(toroa, Black-browed Mollymawk)

DESCRIPTION 'Lesser' dark-backed albatross (also known as 'mollymawks'). Head and body white, upperwings sooty-black and underwings white with black border. Heavy

orange bill pinker towards tip; iris dark brown with narrow black stripe extending behind it. Juveniles grey on nape with brown, black-tipped bill. **DISTRIBUTION** Small numbers breed on Antipodes and Campbell Islands. Regular visitor to SI waters in winter, sometimes further N. Circumpolar. **HABITS AND HABITAT** Gregarious feeder; diet of fish, squid and krill. If threatened during nesting, adults and chicks sometimes eject stinky oily liquid from the stomach at the intruder. **CONSERVATION** Native/Colonizer. Most numerous albatross, with up to three million individuals globally. Perhaps only 150 pairs locally.

Adult

Campbell Island Albatross (e)

■ *Thalassarche impavida* 78–90cm; WS 210–246cm
(Campbell Mollymawk)

DESCRIPTION Once considered conspecific with the Black-browed Albatross (above), identified by its honey-coloured iris. Large bill orange going pinker towards tip, with

triangular black smudge going through eye. Underwing broadly bordered in black with smudging on to white inner patch. Juveniles nearly indistinguishable between species. **DISTRIBUTION** Unique to subantarctic Campbell Islands. Fairly regular visitor to mainland NZ waters. **HABITS AND HABITAT** Prey often caught via diving or surface seizing. Colony calls consist of long, ominous wails and croaks, combined with bill clacking typical of albatrosses. **CONSERVATION** Endemic/ Naturally Uncommon. Breeding grounds secure, but anticipated threats to all seabirds (food availability, plastic ingestion and fisheries bycatch) will come into play in future.

Adults

Buller's Albatross ■ *Thalassarche bulleri* 76–82cm; WS 200–213cm ⓔ
(Buller's Mollymawk)

DESCRIPTION ssp. *platei* (Northern), *bulleri* (Southern). Standout albatross smaller than most. Head dusky-grey aside from silvery crown, going darker on to mantle, then into sooty-black upperwings. Underwings mostly white bordered in black, thicker along leading edge. Rump and underside clean white; tail black. Bill most striking feature, glossy black on sides with yellow plates along top and bottom. On face, black marking goes through dark brown eye and white partial eye-ring, giving stern appearance. Legs and webbed feet pale pink. Nominate southern subspecies differs by lighter head, more diffuse pale crown and thicker yellow patches on bill. Immature birds paler on face with dull brown bill tipped in black. **DISTRIBUTION** Southern subspecies breeds on Tini Heke/The Snares and Solander Islands off Southland. Northern subspecies breeds mainly in Chatham Islands, with small population at Three Kings Islands off Northland. Commonly encountered in waters around mainland NZ. **HABITS AND HABITAT** Varied diet includes fish, squid, tunicates and discards from fishing vessels. Southern subspecies unusual among albatrosses in nesting under tall, dense vegetation. This can involve up to 100m of walking from forest edge, as birds cannot land or take off under the canopy. Mostly silent at sea but gives brays, growls and wails during courtship displays. **CONSERVATION** Endemic/Naturally Uncommon.

Adult Northern species

Adult Southern species

White-capped Albatross ■ *Thalassarche cauta* 90–100cm; WS 220–256cm

(toroa, Shy Mollymawk)

DESCRIPTION ssp. *steadi* (*New Zealand*), *cauta* (Tasmanian) Typical albatross; white with slate-grey upperwings. Light grey face with small black patch around eye. Large greyish

bill with yellow tip diagnostic; orange gape often concealed. Rump white and tail black. Feet dull pink. Juveniles greyer than adults around head and nape, and have dark-tipped beige bill. Tasmanian birds rare vagrants; usually have yellower bills. **DISTRIBUTION** Breeds in Auckland Islands with some at Antipodes. Common in waters off mainland NZ; more numerous further south. **HABITS**

Adult

AND HABITAT Approximately 20 per cent of

population migrates to Indian Ocean after breeding, while most birds stay relatively local. Opportunistic surface feeder, often following boats. Makes a nasal screech. **CONSERVATION** Native/Declining. Suffered highest local bycatch rate of all albatrosses in 2004–2007.

Immature

Indian Yellow-nosed Albatross

■ *Thalassarche carteri* 70–80cm; WS 180–215cm

(Indian Ocean Yellow-nosed Mollymawk)

DESCRIPTION Smallest albatross, gleaming white with long black bill, yellow along top (culmen) and red at tip. Long, slender wings and rounded tail black, along with smudge across eye, giving stern expression. Underwings white with thin dark edge. Bill black on

immatures. **DISTRIBUTION** At least four pairs breed on small islands around Rēkohu/Chathams; very rarely encountered around mainland NZ. Rests on subantarctic islands in Indian Ocean, but disperses widely throughout Southern Ocean when not breeding. **HABITS AND HABITAT** Typical albatross; lives at sea, foraging predominantly for fish. Nasal chatter call. **CONSERVATION** Native/ Colonizer. Regular around mainland in 1980s (particularly Hauraki Gulf). Fisheries bycatch has resulted in a considerable decline since.

Adult

Chatham Island Albatross

■ *Thalassarche eremita* 90cm; WS 220cm ⓔ
(Chatham Mollymawk)

DESCRIPTION Easily recognized by dark grey head, striking eye-patch, and vivid yellow bill with black spot near tip. Broad wings white underneath with narrow dark trailing edge, and all black above. Black-brown mantle contrasts with white rump and underparts. **DISTRIBUTION** Breeds only on The Pyramid, an isolated rock stack located in SE of Rēkohu/Chatham Islands. Rarely recorded around mainland NZ. **HABITS AND HABITAT** Birds stay relatively local except in winter, when most move to waters off Peru and Chile. **CONSERVATION** Endemic/ Naturally Uncommon. Single breeding location poses risk to survival; 282 chicks translocated over five years (2013–2018) to Point Gap on Chatham Island were unsuccessful in starting new colony.

Adult

Salvin's Albatross ■ *Thalassarche salvini* 90–100cm; WS 250cm ⓔ
(Salvin's Mollymawk)

DESCRIPTION Medium-sized albatross with grey head, throat and neck; silver crown and black eye-shadow. Robust beige bill with pale upper ridge and dark spot at tip of lower mandible. Upperwings dark brown; underwings white bordered in black. Tail and back dark grey. **DISTRIBUTION** Main breeding site is Bounty Islands as well as Western Chain Islets of Tini Heke/Snares Islands. Commonly encountered in waters around mainland NZ, more so S of Cook Strait. **HABITS AND HABITAT** While ungainly on land, stiff, narrow wings allow it to soar and glide with ease. Main call a nasal chattering. **CONSERVATION** Endemic/ Nationally Critical. Longline fisheries and trawlers responsible for high proportion of mortality at sea.

Adult

Grey-headed Albatross
■ *Thalassarche chrysostoma* 80–82cm; WS 180–220cm
(Grey-headed Mollymawk)

DESCRIPTION Albatross with distinctive, ashy-grey head, transitioning into black upperwings. White underwings bordered messily in deep black, noticeably thicker along

leading edge. Rump appears stark white against black tail. Bill mostly black with yellow along top and bottom and red-tinted hook. Juveniles have entirely black bills and darker heads. **DISTRIBUTION** Aound 6,500 pairs breed on Campbell Island in NZ, rarely visiting mainland waters. Circumpolar. **HABITS AND HABITAT** Often nests on grassy coastal cliffs. Gives braying and chattering calls during nesting. Deep water specialist. **CONSERVATION** Native/Nationally Vulnerable. Increasing distance between Polar Front feeding grounds and breeding grounds has shown to negatively impact populations.

Adults at nest

Light-mantled Sooty Albatross
■ *Phoebetria palpebrata* 78–90cm; WS 180–220cm
(toroa pango)

DESCRIPTION Elegant, striking albatross with atypical grey-brown plumage, palest on back. Both pointed wings and wedge-shaped tail long and narrow, aiding rapid flight. Head blackish with partial white eye-ring. Bill black with pale blue stripe along lower mandible.
DISTRIBUTION Rarely ventures to waters around NZ mainland, breeding further S on Auckland, Campbell and Antipodes Islands. Occurs throughout Southern Ocean.

HABITS AND HABITAT Pairs breed once every two years and perform graceful synchronized courtship flight. Forages squid, fish and crustaceans as far S as Antarctic pack ice. Colony call a wheezy shriek. **CONSERVATION** Native/ Nationally Vulnerable. Bycatch mortality from longline fisheries known to be major factor.

Southern Giant Petrel ■ *Macronectes giganteus* 86–100cm; WS 185–205cm
(pāngurunguru)

DESCRIPTION Large, heavy-bodied seabird with huge yellow bill, tipped light green. Adult dark morph mottled brown, with whitish from face outwards as it ages. Rare white morph (10 per cent of birds) wholly white with odd brown feathers. Iris pale, legs grey-brown. Dark-eyed juveniles entirely sooty-brown, lightening with age. Rounded head, broad wings and hump back distinctive in flight. Face can be bloody after scavenging.

DISTRIBUTION Uncommon winter migrant to NZ waters. Nearest colony is on subantarctic Macquarie Island, Australia. Circumpolar. **HABITS AND HABITAT** Very aggressive predator that often kills and eats other seabirds. Gives noisy growls, whinnies and bill snaps during feeding frenzies. **CONSERVATION** Native/Migrant.

Adult white morph

Juvenile

Northern Giant Petrel
■ *Macronectes halli* 80–95cm; WS 150–210cm
(pāngurunguru)

DESCRIPTION Bulky seabird with huge, pale orange bill, dark reddish-brown at tip (most reliable way to identify species). Adults mottled brown, with birds lightening from face outwards with age. Juveniles entirely dark brown, including iris (silver in adults). **DISTRIBUTION** Regularly seen off mainland NZ coast and in surrounding waters. Breeds locally at Auckland, Campbell, Antipodes and Chatham Islands, and across Southern Ocean. **HABITS AND HABITAT** Similar to the Southern Giant Petrel (above) but much more common. Opportunistic diet of fish, squid, carrion such as dead birds, seals and even whales, which attract huge aggregations. Also follows vessels for any potential discards. **CONSERVATION** Native/Recovering.

Immature

Adult

Cape Petrel ▪ *Daption capense* 35–42cm; WS 80–90cm ⓔ
(karetai hurukoko, Pintado Petrel)

DESCRIPTION ssp. *capense* (Antarctic) *australe (Snares)*. Distinctive stocky petrel with highly contrasting black and white plumage. Back forms chequered pattern, which continues on to upperwings in Antarctic subspecies. Snares subspecies has black upperwings with distinct white patches and darker backs. Stubby black bill. White tail tipped in black. **DISTRIBUTION** Summer breeder common in NZ waters, more prolific S of Cook Strait. Endemic subspecies nests on Snares, Auckland, Antipode, Bounty and Chatham Islands. Widespread throughout Southern Ocean and around Antarctica coast. **HABITS AND HABITAT** Social species, attracted to feeding frenzies and fishing boats, where it can form immense squabbling flocks. Prefers krill and amphipods; also take offal and burley. Call a noisy staccato chirping. **CONSERVATION** Native/ Naturally Uncommon.

Snares subspecies   *Antarctic subspecies*

Snares subspecies

Antarctic Fulmar ▪ *Fulmarus glacialoides* 45–50cm; WS 114–120cm
(Southern Fulmar)

DESCRIPTION Stocky, gull-like petrel. White overall with blue-grey upperwings and back. Outer wing black with white panels. Underwings and short, rounded tail white. Large bill pink, with dark tip and blue nasal tubes. Eyes dark and feet greyish-pink. Soars on broad, stiff wings. **DISTRIBUTION** Uncommon visitor to NZ deep waters in May–Dec, most often seen singly off Kaikoura and Otago. Circumpolar breeder. **HABITS AND HABITAT** Nests constructed in dense colonies on cliff faces and steep rocky slopes. Highly nomadic pelagic species. Diet of fish, krill and small cephalopods. Call a croaky rattle. **CONSERVATION** Native/Migrant. Population stable although appears to be breeding later in response to diminishing sea-ice around Antarctica.

White-headed Petrel
▪ *Pterodroma lessonii* 40–46cm; WS 109cm

DESCRIPTION Large white seabird with distinctive dark grey wings both above and below. Head white with smudgy black patch around eye; back and mantle mid-grey. Worn birds have greyish head and collar. Long, narrow wings somewhat reflective underneath. Stout black bill strongly hooked, and legs pink. **DISTRIBUTION** Rare winter visitor to waters of mainland NZ. Breeds locally on Auckland and Antipodes Islands during summer. Also on French subantarctic islands. Circumpolar occurrence in Southern Ocean. **HABITS AND HABITAT** Active nocturnally at breeding grounds. After coming inshore quickly retreats under vegetation or into underground burrow. Call a high-pitched *si-si-si* or low groaning typical of Pterodroma petrels. **CONSERVATION** Native/Not Threatened.

Grey-faced Petrel ■ *Pterodroma gouldi* 38–43cm; WS 97–102cm
(ōi)

DESCRIPTION Large, stocky gadfly petrel (named for rapid soaring flight, as if evading gadflies), with uniformly dark grey-brown plumage. Diagnostic pale face centred around base of bill and forehead varies in extent; darker patch in front of large brown eye. Heavy, stout bill black with sharp hook at tip. Legs and webbed feet also black. Underwing can appear metallic in strong light. **DISTRIBUTION** Endemic breeder with colonies scattered around coast of upper NI, on Three Kings, and islands in Hauraki Gulf and Bay of Plenty. Ranges throughout Tasman Sea and S Pacific. **HABITS AND HABITAT** Breeding colonies often under coastal forest on headlands and peninsulas. Very active at night, with birds calling, displaying and prospecting for burrows. One white egg laid in Jun–Jul and incubated by both parents. Chicks hatch about 55 days later. Most do not fledge until mid-summer. Generalist feeder, readily taking a variety of fish, crustaceans and cephalopods.

Usually dives down to 5m depth; occasionally as far as 20m. Call heard most often in colonies reminiscent of a squeaky wheel. **CONSERVATION** Endemic/Not Threatened. Monitored mainland populations often do better with predator control and artificial nesting boxes.

Chatham Island Tāiko ■ *Pterodroma magentae* 39–42cm; WS 102cm ⓔ
(tchaik in Moriori, Magenta Petrel)

DESCRIPTION Once-mythical seabird. White plumage below with shiny, dark grey head and upperparts giving hooded appearance. Dark underwing lighter on trailing edge. Paler around bill, with dark eye-patch. Stout black bill sharply hooked. Legs pink; toes black. **DISTRIBUTION** Breeds only in SW corner of Rēkohu/Chatham Island. Moves widely over S Pacific Ocean in winter. **HABITS AND HABITAT** Nests in 2–6m-deep burrows in peaty soil under dense native forest. Long, moaning call. **CONSERVATION** Endemic/ Nationally Critical. First specimen shot in S Pacific from Italian warship in 1867. Presumed extinct until rediscovery on Chatham Island 111 years later. About 50 pairs remain with intensive conservation efforts underway.

Kermadec Petrel ■ *Pterodroma neglecta* 38cm; WS 92cm
(pia koia)

DESCRIPTION ssp. *neglecta*. Thickset subtropical seabird with three plumage types. Dark morph dull brown with grey on face and belly. Intermediate generally greyish overall with white belly. Pale morph mostly white with dusky crown, and dark wings and back. All birds have stubby black bill, white wing-flashes and short, squared tail. Legs pink to black. **DISTRIBUTION** Breeds on Kermadec Islands, as well as Lord Howe and Norfolk Islands, Australia, and other S Pacific Islands. Straggles to mainland NZ. **HABITS AND HABITAT** Resemblance to skuas may help in mobbing other seabirds for prey. Call a noisy croon heard only in colonies. **CONSERVATION** Native/Naturally Uncommon.

Dark morph

Pale morph

White-necked Petrel

■ *Pterodroma cervicalis* 43cm; WS 95–105cm
(White-naped Petrel)

DESCRIPTION Large seabird with long
wings and tail. Dark 'M' shape traverses
scalloped grey upperparts; white underwing
edged dark brown. Blackish cap contrasts
with white on forehead, throat, nape and
underparts. Heavy black bill hooked at tip.
Graceful, soaring flight. **DISTRIBUTION**
Breeds on Kermadec Islands and Norfolk
Island of Australia. Rare visitor to waters of
N NZ. Migrates to NW Pacific (off Japan)
after breeding. **HABITS AND HABITAT**
Strongly pelagic, preferring warmer tropical
waters. Utters a variety of raucously
high-pitched honking and peeping calls.
CONSERVATION Native/Relict. Raoul
Island colony was exterminated by rats
and cats by 1914; since the island became
predator free in 2006 there is hope that it
will return naturally.

Black-winged Petrel

■ *Pterodroma nigripennis* 28–30cm; WS 63–71cm
(karetai kapa mangu)

DESCRIPTION Narrow-winged petrel. Mid-
grey above with indistinct white supercilium,
speckled forehead and black over eye. Dark
'M' shape spans upperwings and rump, faded in
worn birds. Thick black border to underwing
diagnostic, seen clearly while in flight. Clean
white below except for pale grey collar.
Black bill stubby, legs pink and feet black.
DISTRIBUTION Breeds in small colonies on
islands of N NZ; most on Kermadec Islands
and around SW Pacific. Migrates eastwards
across Pacific after breeding. **HABITS AND
HABITAT** Unusually, visits breeding grounds
both day and night. Feeds on crustaceans and
squid. Sharp, squealing calls given at colonies.
CONSERVATION Native/Not Threatened.

Mottled Petrel ■ *Pterodroma inexpectata* 33–35cm; WS 74–85cm ⓔ
(kōrure)

DESCRIPTION Stocky, medium-sized petrel. Head grey with white on face, throat and breast. Back and upperwings scaled grey with faint, darker 'M' shape. Underwing white with bold black markings and dark trailing edge. Dirty grey belly diagnostic, vent white. Small black bill. **DISTRIBUTION** Uncommon off mainland NZ, most regularly around Otago and Rakiura/Stewart Island. Most breed on Whenua Hou/Codfish Island and Tini Heke/The Snares. Migrates to N Pacific during spring. **HABITS AND HABITAT** Prey such as squid, krill and lantern fish is picked from the water's surface in flight. Call a nasal, repeated *ti-ti-ti-ti* in addition to low growl. **CONSERVATION** Endemic/Relict. Chicks translocated to Hawke's Bay, 24km from ocean, have returned to breed.

Soft-plumaged Petrel
■ *Pterodroma mollis* 32–37cm; WS 83–95cm

DESCRIPTION Typical petrel with diagnostic dark underwings. Head and collar dark grey with black eye-patch, and variable amounts of white on throat and forehead. Upperwings and back slate-grey with faint 'M' marking. Underside clean white. Stubby black bill with bulbous hooked tip. Legs pink; feet black. Rare sooty-grey dark morph not yet recorded in NZ. **DISTRIBUTION** Rare visitor to waters of mainland NZ. Breeds in small numbers on Antipodes Islands, and in S Atlantic and Indian Oceans. **HABITS AND HABITAT** Solitary while at sea. Nests under dense ferns and tussock grasses. High-pitched, whining call not unlike that of a dog heard in colonies. **CONSERVATION** Native/Naturally Uncommon.

Cook's Petrel ■ *Pterodroma cookii* 25–30cm; WS 65cm ⓔ
(tītī)

DESCRIPTION ssp. *cookii* (Northern), *orientalis* (Southern). Typical Cookilaria petrel (subgroup of *Pterodroma*). Mid-grey above with dark 'M' shape extending across back. Underwings white with thin dark border; underside pure white with diffuse grey shoulder tabs. Large eye hidden in black patch, and forehead white with prominent white supercilium. Bill black with hooked tip, and legs greyish with dark webbing. Direct weaving flight interrupted by high arcs into the sky. Larger, lighter and longer winged than very similar Pycroft's Petrel (opposite), as well as having shorter tail and longer bill. **DISTRIBUTION** Breeding grounds consist of Hauturu/Little Barrier and Aotea/Great Barrier Islands in N, and Whenua Hou/Codfish Island in S. Common in Hauraki Gulf during summer and waters around NZ. Migrates throughout wider Pacific Ocean after breeding season. **HABITS AND HABITAT** Favoured sites for colonies are under mature forest on mountain peaks and ridges. Active nocturnally on land, especially during stormy periods and the new moon. Breeds Sep–Apr. As in all petrels, only a single white egg is laid. Birds feed singly or in loose flocks, predominately on small squid, and have capacity to dive up to 20m in pursuit of them. Call a distinctive nasal *meep-meep-meep*, heard frequently from birds flying overland to colonies and during squabbles at sea. **CONSERVATION** Endemic/Relict. Attempts to re-establish colonies in fenced predator-proofed areas on mainland in Hawke's Bay show early signs of success.

Pycroft's Petrel ■ *Pterodroma pycrofti* 26–28cm; WS 53cm

DESCRIPTION Small, slender petrel with pointed wings and tapering tail. Dusky-grey above with prominent neck-tabs and blackish 'M' shape above. Underwings white with black edging; pure white below. Eye-patch slightly darker, and forehead speckled white with variable brow-stripe. Small, stubby bill black; feet lilac. Rare tropical **Gould's Petrel** *P. leucoptera* has dark brown hood. **DISTRIBUTION** Breeds on islands off NE NZ, including Poor Knights, Hen and Chickens, and Mercury Island. Frequents waters of Northland and Coromandel, and migrates to N Pacific during winter. **HABITS AND HABITAT** Forages offshore on small squids and crustaceans. Call a repetitive *si-si-si-si* coupled with a whiny purr. **CONSERVATION** Endemic/Recovering.

Chatham Petrel ■ *Pterodroma axillaris* 30cm; WS 63–71cm
(ranguru)

DESCRIPTION Head grey with dark smudge over eye. Back and upperwings also grey, with typical darker 'M' shape. Underside white. Underwing white with bold black marking extending from armpit towards leading edge. Stubby black bill. **DISTRIBUTION** Population restricted to 218ha Rangatira Island, with new ones being established on Rekohu/Chatham and Pitt Islands. Rarely seen at sea. Migrates to South American waters after breeding. **HABITS AND HABITAT** Birds land within metres of the same burrow each season. To leave they climb trees and take off above the canopy. **CONSERVATION** Endemic/Nationally Vulnerable. Broad-billed Prions (p. 97) evict birds from burrows and destroy eggs and kill chicks; special doors installed to prevent this.

Westland Petrel
■ *Procellaria westlandica* 50–55cm; WS 135–140cm ⓔ
(tāiko)

DESCRIPTION Robust brownish-black seabird. Head rounded and wings long; wing undersides can appear reflective. Large bill ivory in colour, outlined in black with bulbous black tip. Legs and feet black. **DISTRIBUTION** Only breeding grounds are in foothills of Paparoa National Park in West Coast, SI. Regularly seen in mainland waters, especially Cook Strait to Otago. Migrates to South American waters after breeding. **HABITS AND HABITAT** Mostly solitary at sea, feeding via surface seizing and diving. Witnessing birds returning to colony at dusk near Punakaiki is a spectacular experience. Moans and rattling shrieks often heard in colony. **CONSERVATION** Endemic/ Naturally Uncommon.

Adult

Black Petrel
■ *Procellaria parkinsoni* 46cm; WS 110–115cm ⓔ
(tāiko, takoketai, Parkinson's Petrel)

DESCRIPTION Medium-sized petrel with slight build and overall sooty-black plumage. Tail pointed and wings long; undersides of primaries reflective. Bill pale yellow with black between plates and at tip. Legs and feet black. **DISTRIBUTION** Breeding restricted to Hauturu/Little Barrier and Aotea/Great Barrier Islands. Regularly seen in mainland waters, especially Hauraki Gulf. At sea ranges from Australian to C American coasts in winter and spring. **HABITS AND HABITAT** Mostly solitary when pelagic, but birds congregate around cetaceans (whales and dolphins) in feeding frenzies. Low, clacking call heard in colony. **CONSERVATION** Endemic/Nationally Vulnerable. One of many species extirpated from mainland by rats, cats, feral pigs and mustelids.

White-chinned Petrel

■ *Procellaria aequinoctialis* 51–58cm; WS 134–147cm
(karetai kauae mā)

DESCRIPTION Large, heavy-bodied seabird with brown-black plumage and white chin-patch that varies from a few white feathers to most of throat (rare). Wings long and broad, and tail short and wedge shaped. Stout bill overall pale yellow outlined in black. Feet black. **DISTRIBUTION** In NZ breeds on subantarctic Auckland, Campbell and Antipodes Islands, as well as South Georgia and Kerguelen Islands among others. Regular visitor to mainland waters Sep–Apr, especially south of Cook Strait. **HABITS AND HABITAT** Pelagic forager on fish, squid and salps, and also takes handouts from passing fishing vessels, which it follows. Calls range from drawn-out squeals, to low growling and bill clapping. **CONSERVATION** Native/Not Threatened.

Grey Petrel

■ *Procellaria cinerea* 50cm; WS 115–130cm
(kuia)

DESCRIPTION Fairly large petrel. Dusky grey colouring above, going darker on to face, wings and short tail. Back, rump and upperwing feathers scaled, and underwings dark. Pale underside with smudgy border. Bill light green-grey with blackish tip and edges. Legs and feet pinkish. **DISTRIBUTION** Breeds on subantarctic Antipodes and Campbell Islands, and in S Atlantic and Indian Oceans. Can be seen in deep water around NZ in Jun–Oct, particularly Otago. Spends summer off S America. **HABITS AND HABITAT** Colonial breeder, nesting in 1–3m-deep burrows on steep, well-vegetated slopes. Winter breeder, with one white egg laid in March–April. Call a quavering, staccato drone coupled with low moaning. **CONSERVATION** Native/Naturally Uncommon.

Blue Petrel ■ *Halobaena caerulea*
28–30cm; WS 66cm

DESCRIPTION Striking seabird, icy-blue above with dark, curved markings across each wing. White below, on face and forehead, with distinctive sooty cap reaching down to form partial collar. Bill black and feet blue. Broad, white-tipped tail diagnostic even with poor views. **DISTRIBUTION** Rare winter migrant to NZ waters, with nearest colony on subantarctic Macquarie Island of Australia. Also breeds in S Atlantic and Indian Oceans. **HABITS AND HABITAT** The bridge between petrels and prions, often flocking inconspicuously with the latter. Strongly pelagic, with preference for cold, deep water. Can be found beach-wrecked on W coast beaches in winter, especially after storm events. Silent at sea. **CONSERVATION** Native/Migrant.

Thin-billed Prion ■ *Pachyptila belcheri* 25–28cm; WS 56cm
(Slender-billed Prion, korotangi)

DESCRIPTION Dainty prion. Blue-grey above with faint 'M' shape across back and bold shoulder-tabs and narrow black tip to tail. Clean white on underside. Facial features

include broad white brow, lores and throat, and thin, dusky eye-stripe. Small, narrow bill blue edged dark, and legs blue. **DISTRIBUTION** Rarely seen in waters off NZ, but breeds in huge numbers around S tip of South America and on Kerguelen Islands. **HABITS AND HABITAT** At sea feeds over cold water in mixed flocks with other prion species. Often beach-wrecked sometimes in large numbers. Diet mainly zooplankton but also takes small fish, squid and krill, foraged by surface seizing, shallow dives and hydroplaning. **CONSERVATION** Native/Migrant.

Antarctic Prion ■ *Pachyptila desolata* 25–28cm; WS 58–66cm
(totorore)

DESCRIPTION Typical prion, or 'whalebird', named for lamellae fringe in bill. Blue-grey above with dusky 'M' shape, distinct shoulder-tabs and small black tip to rounded tail. Dusky eye-mask and white supercilium on face. Bill pale blue, can be big or small (hindering ID). Very similar **Salvin's Prion** *P. salvini* a rare winter migrant, with larger and darker bill. **DISTRIBUTION** Infrequently seen in waters around mainland NZ, breeding on subantarctic Auckland Islands. Also throughout Southern Ocean. **HABITS AND HABITAT** Obtains food through hydroplaning, where bird flies while skimming its bill in the water. Silent at sea; radio-like chattering heard in colonies. **CONSERVATION** Native/Naturally Uncommon.

Broad-billed Prion ■ *Pachyptila vittata* 28–30cm; WS 57–66cm
(pararā)

DESCRIPTION Small, stocky seabird with enormous blackish, boat-shaped bill. Blue-grey colouring with faint 'M' above and pale below; distinct shoulder-tabs. Wedge-shaped tail tipped in black. Appears large headed, with dark eye-mask and crown, prominent white brow and steep forehead. **DISTRIBUTION** Uncommon in waters around mainland NZ aside from nearby colonies; islands of Fiordland and Rakiura/Stewart Island, Snares Island and Chatham Islands. Circumpolar and sedentary. **HABITS AND HABITAT** All prion species occur beach wrecked on W coast beaches. Silent at sea, but gives excited croaks in colonies. **CONSERVATION** Native/Relict.

Fairy Prion ■ *Pachyptila turtur*
23–28cm; WS 56–60cm
(tītī wainui)

DESCRIPTION ssp. *turtur, eatoni* (Subantarctic). Cornflour-blue with white belly and underwings. 'M' marking above, matching broad black band at tail-tip. White supercilium and grey eye-patch. Short bill blue-grey with black lining, and legs pale blue. Varies in plumage and structure but Subantarctic birds generally paler with shorter bills. **DISTRIBUTION** Abundant in waters around NZ; widespread breeder from Poor Knights Islands S to subantarctic, with key sites in Marlborough Sounds, around Rakiura/Stewart and Rēkohu/Chatham Islands. Also in S Atlantic and Indian Oceans. **HABITS AND HABITAT** Frequently encountered in huge flocks at sea, often in association with shoals of fish. Gives croons and chatters on breeding grounds. **CONSERVATION** Native/Relict.

Fulmar Prion ■ *Pachyptila crassirostris* 26cm; WS 60cm

DESCRIPTION ssp. *crassirostris, flemingi* (Lesser). Nearly indistinguishable from the Fairy Prion (above). Chunkier bill and larger nail; less-defined but variable facial markings; bluer underparts and blacker tail-tip. May also have more towering flight pattern. **DISTRIBUTION** Found on Tini Heke/Snares, Auckland Islands and Bounty Islands; rarely identified far from breeding islands, with little known about pelagic range. **HABITS AND HABITAT** Nominate subspecies unusual as it is active in colonies during daylight, squabbling, vocalizing and performing courtship displays. Prefers to nest in caves, crevices, rock piles and scree slopes, rather than in burrows. **CONSERVATION** Endemic/Naturally Uncommon. Split of Chatham endemic **Pyramid Prion** *P. pyramidalis* proposed in 2022 based on genetic differences.

Pyramid Prion

Fulmar Prion

Common Diving Petrel
■ *Pelecanoides urinatrix* 20–23cm; WS 33–38cm
(kuaka)

DESCRIPTION ssp. *urinatrix* (*Northern*), *chathamensis* (*Southern*), *exsul* (*Subantarctic*). Small, densely built seabird resembling a miniature penguin on the water. Glossy black with greenish tinge above, and whitish below with grey-smudged underwings, breast (variably) and face. Flight feathers and tail dark grey. Stubby bill black and feet blue with black webbing. Flies with purpose on short, whirring wingbeats. **DISTRIBUTION** Breeds sparsely on islands surrounding mainland NZ as well as Rēkohu/ Chatham Islands, Tini Heke/Snares Islands and Antipodes Islands, with an estimated 1,000,000 pairs in region. Circumpolar. **HABITS AND HABITAT** Predominately crustacean-based prey caught via wing-propelled diving; capable of reaching 60m depth. Main call a sweet, rising 'croon'. **CONSERVATION** Native/Relict.

Whenua Hou Diving Petrel
■ *Pelecanoides georgicus* 20cm; WS 30–35cm
(kuaka whenua hou, South Georgian Diving Petrel)

DESCRIPTION ssp. *georgicus, whenuahouensis*. Short-winged seabird, glossy black above and pure white below. Face dark, with greyish ear-coverts forming faint crescent. Prominent white scapulars run down back. Flight feathers and slightly forked tail dark grey; underwings and undertail white. Broad-based bill black; lower mandible and legs cobalt-blue. **DISTRIBUTION** Restricted today to Whenua Hou/Codfish Island W of Rakiura/Stewart Island. Other subspecies on South Georgia. **HABITS AND HABITAT** Breeds exclusively in burrows on sparsely vegetated coastal sand dunes. Produces series of 5–10 squeaky, undulating croons, and short, rising note while flying over colony. **CONSERVATION** Native/Nationally Critical, with 200 adults remaining. Whenua Hou is predator-free and has limited access, but storm events and habitat erosion still threaten survival.

Wilson's Storm Petrel ■ *Oceanites oceanicus* 18cm; WS 38–42cm

DESCRIPTION ssp. *exasperatus*. Small black seabird with steep forehead and tiny black bill. White rump and flanks stand out in flight, as well as long, slender black legs with

yellow webbing. Wings broad, and black tail distinctly squared. **DISTRIBUTION** Uncommon passage migrant to waters around NZ, most often seen in spring and autumn. Breeds in huge numbers around Antarctic coast and migrates to northern seas for austral winter. **HABITS AND HABITAT** Nests in ice-free rocky crevices and small burrows in soft earth. Strictly nocturnal on land to avoid detection by predatory gulls and skuas. Birds forage beyond pack ice in cold, deep water for small fish, squid and planktonic invertebrates. **CONSERVATION** Native/Migrant.

Black-bellied Storm Petrel ■ *Fregetta tropica* 20cm; WS 46cm
(takahikare-rangi)

DESCRIPTION Small, compact seabird with steep forehead and tiny black bill. Head and chest black. Underside and rump white with black line running down centre of belly (sometimes broken or absent). Pointed wings dark brown, interior of underwings pale. Long legs and feet black, and rounded tail. **DISTRIBUTION** Circumpolar. Breeds locally on subantarctic Auckland and Antipodes islands. Uncommon in mainland waters, particularly seen off Otago and Rakiura/Stewart Island. **HABITS AND HABITAT** Foraging technique involves skipping off waves asymmetrically using one leg and dipping bill into the water, taking aquatic invertebrates and small squids. **CONSERVATION** Native/Not Threatened.

White-bellied Storm Petrel ■ *Fregetta grallaria* 20cm; WS 42cm

DESCRIPTION ssp. *grallaria* (Tasmanian). Small seabird with black hood, tiny bill, and dark brown wings and tail. Belly, rump and centre of underwings typically clean white. Rarely, birds have light streaking on flanks; some can even appear completely black. Long legs, webs and claws black. **DISTRIBUTION** Breeds on Kermadec Islands, as well as Lord Howe Island in Australia. Ranges at sea to N and E of breeding grounds; very rare around mainland NZ. Occurs throughout tropical S Pacific and S Atlantic. **HABITS AND HABITAT** When flying, often drags one foot through the water, skipping and bouncing off the surface. Strictly nocturnal when on land, where it gives soft, twittering calls. **CONSERVATION** Native/Nationally Endangered. Around 700 may live in NZ.

New Zealand Storm Petrel ■ *Fregetta maoriana* 17–20cm; WS 46cm
(takahikare-raro)

DESCRIPTION Dainty black seabird with white belly covered in dark striations varying in intensity. Short, drooping bill, long legs and webbed feet also black. Stark white rump stands out in flight, with birds stopping in mid-air to dance on the water's surface. **DISTRIBUTION** Always seen well offshore around NE NI, most frequently in Hauraki Gulf. Breeding only on Hauturu/Little Barrier Island. Vagrant to Australia. **HABITS AND HABITAT** Nests in small, crevice-like burrows under native forest. Solitary while feeding at sea, but congregates in groups of up to 100 birds over chum slicks behind boats. **CONSERVATION** Endemic/Nationally Vulnerable. Presumed extinct. Dramatic rediscovery in 2003 with breeding grounds confirmed in 2013. Low frequency of banded bird re-sightings suggests that thousands of individuals exist.

White-faced Storm Petrel

▪ *Pelagodroma marina* 18–21cm; WS 42–43cm
(takahikare)

DESCRIPTION ssp. *maoriana* (New Zealand), *dulciae* (Australian). Small, lightly built seabird. Predominately grey-brown with white underparts. Distinct white brow and face, with dark grey eyes and shoulder-patches. Narrow, downcurved bill and long, slender black legs with yellow webbing on feet. Birds bounce off water in arcs with their legs dangling and broad wings held high. **DISTRIBUTION** Common in NZ waters in Aug–Apr, breeding on small islands from Northland to Rakiura/Stewart Island and the Chathams. Other subspecies in all oceans. **HABITS AND HABITAT** Breeding limited to pest-free islands; even mice cause issues. Both parents responsible for incubation and chick rearing. Small flocks can be seen at sea. Main call heard in colonies is gentle piping. **CONSERVATION** Native/Relict.

Kermadec Storm Petrel ▪ *Pelagodroma albiclunis* 20cm; WS 42cm

DESCRIPTION Identical to the White-faced Storm Petrel (above), except it has white rump and smaller grey shoulder-tabs. Juveniles have white panels on upperwings.

DISTRIBUTION Only known from around Kermadec Islands, where it breeds on Haszard Island. Migrates elsewhere December–April; details unknown. One record from Australia. **HABITS AND HABITAT** Highly pelagic; observed at sea near sea mounts in proximity to upwelling and bountiful food sources. Lays single egg in burrow in August. **CONSERVATION** Endemic/Nationally Critical, with estimated 100–300 pairs. Kermadecs made predator free in 2006, so should hopefully recover and increase. Main threat will be nest-site competition from other seabirds. Sometimes regarded as subspecies.

Grey-backed Storm Petrel ■ *Garrodia nereis* 16–19cm; WS 39cm
(reoreo)

DESCRIPTION Tiny, delicate seabird. Dark grey head and upperwings. White underwings bordered in grey darker along leading edge. Wing-bars, back, rump and tail light grey, the latter with dark tip. Breast and belly clean white. Black bill very stubby. **DISTRIBUTION**
Breeds on Chatham, Antipodes, Campbell and Auckland Islands. Infrequent visitor to waters around mainland, most often seen off Kaikoura, Otago and Southland. Possibly also breeds on remote islands in Fiordland. Circumpolar but rarely ventures far from nesting sites. **HABITS AND HABITAT** Nests under dense vegetation such as pohuehue, tussocks and flax. Call heard on land a repetitive, wheezy *chirp*. **CONSERVATION** Native/Relict. Vulnerable to predation from Brown Skua (p. 60) around colonies.

Buller's Shearwater ■ *Ardenna bulleri* 43–47cm; WS 96–102cm
(rako)

DESCRIPTION Large, slender shearwater with all-white underparts and cheeks. Dusky mid-grey to brown upperparts. Distinctive dark brown, 'M'-shaped marking above matches contrasting cap and wedge-shaped tail. Long, dark-tipped bill and grey legs with pink-
webbed feet. **DISTRIBUTION** Sole breeding grounds on Poor Knights group in Hauraki Gulf. Commonly seen in NZ waters, before migrating throughout Pacific Ocean after breeding season. **HABITS AND HABITAT** Burrows can occur under tree roots, in rock crevices or simply in soil; preference for dense native forest cover above. Birds arrive at dusk in immense, noisy aggregations, crashing through the canopy. Colony call an intense, scratchy wailing. **CONSERVATION** Endemic/Declining. Unanticipated decline in recent years, with bycatch from fisheries a likely contributor.

Wedge-tailed Shearwater ■ *Ardenna pacifica* 46–47cm; WS 97–99cm

DESCRIPTION ssp. *pacifica, chlororhynchus*. Slender tropical shearwater. Plumage dimorphic. Common 'dark' form uniformly chocolate-brown with lighter tips to upperwing feathers. 'Pale' form has soft cream underparts including underwings (more common in N Pacific). Long, thin bill grey, and legs pinkish. Diagnostic long, wedge-shaped tail. **DISTRIBUTION** Breeds on Kermadec Islands; rare visitor to waters off N NZ. Widespread throughout Pacific and Indian Oceans. **HABITS AND HABITAT** Strongly pelagic, with diet mostly of fish; often found feeding in mixed groups with other seabirds or cetaceans. On land calls given are slow, wailing moans. **CONSERVATION** Native/Relict. May be declining due to changing sea temperatures and resulting food availability.

Flesh-footed Shearwater ■ *Ardenna carneipes* 46–48cm; WS 115cm
(toanui)

DESCRIPTION Uniformly chocolate-brown, and can appear shiny after moult. Diagnostic flesh-coloured feet and long, slender dark-tipped bill. Wings long and tail pointed. Immature birds have paler bills and legs. **DISTRIBUTION** Breeds on islands around N NZ

and Cook Strait; regularly seen in surrounding waters. Migrates to N Pacific outside breeding season. Also found around Australia and in Indian Ocean. **HABITS AND HABITAT** Diet mainly fish caught on shallow dives, but can go to maximum depth of 30m. Often sits behind boats in hope of handouts. Gives cat-like wailing call and powerful *oo-oooh*. **CONSERVATION** Native/Relict. Plastic fragments have been seen more regularly in colonies.

Sooty Shearwater ■ *Ardenna grisea* 40–46cm; WS 94–105cm
(tītī)

DESCRIPTION Stocky, medium-sized shearwater with entirely charcoal-coloured plumage, apart from silver flash on underwings. Wings long and narrow, and bill robust but varies in size. **DISTRIBUTION** Breeds on islands all around NZ coast and remote headlands; regularly seen in surrounding waters. Migrates to N Pacific outside breeding season. Also found around Australia and in Indian Ocean. **HABITS AND HABITAT** Congregates in immense flocks at sea. Main call heard nocturnally on breeding grounds a nasal *coo-roo-ah*, repeated with increasing intensity. **CONSERVATION** Native/ Declining. Large chicks, or 'muttonbirds', still harvested traditionally on Tītī Islands around Rakiura/Stewart Island, with an estimated 400,000 taken each year.

Short-tailed Shearwater
■ *Ardenna tenuirostris* 40–45cm; 95–100cm

DESCRIPTION Compact stiff-winged shearwater very similar to Sooty (above). Generally slightly lighter underside, darker underwings, shorter narrow bill (with long tubenose) and rounder head. **DISTRIBUTION** Endemic to Australia, but occurs in waters around NZ during summer and autumn. Migrates to N Pacific and Arctic Ocean in winter. **HABITS AND HABITAT** Forms large rafts, sometimes with dolphins or other seabirds. Piscivorous, diving up to 10m in search of fish, squid and crustaceans. **CONSERVATION** Native/Migrant. Possibly most numerous shearwater, with estimated 23 million globally, but has still shown significant decline in recent years.

Fluttering Shearwater ■ *Puffinus gavia* 32–37cm; WS 76cm (e)
(pakahā)

DESCRIPTION Small seabird with dusky-brown upperparts and white underparts. Dark bill long and slender. Chin white; sometimes with indistinct collar across throat.

Underwings variable, generally whitish with darker flight feathers and axillaries (armpit). White 'saddlebags' extend up between wing and tail. Distinctive switching 'flutter-glide' flight pattern. **DISTRIBUTION** Common around NZ, especially in Hauraki Gulf where majority breeds. Foraging range extends as far as SE Australia. **HABITS AND HABITAT** Faithful nester, often returning to same mate and underground burrow year after year. Enormous flocks congregate inshore during late summer moult. **CONSERVATION** Endemic/Relict. Over-harvesting of prey fish could have serious impacts in the future.

Hutton's Shearwater ■ *Puffinus huttoni* 36–38cm; WS 72–78cm (e)
(kaikōura tītī)

DESCRIPTION Slender seabird, take care to separate from Fluttering (above). Dark brown above and white below with dark 'hood' and smudgy collar across throat. Underwings

mottled brown with diagnostic large black axillary (armpit) wedge. Eye has fine pale ring, feet are pinkish-brown. Narrow bill very long. **DISTRIBUTION** Breeding restricted to Seaward Kaikoura Range in Canterbury, plus a translocated colony to Kaikoura Peninsula. Occurs off E South Island in huge flocks. Migrates to waters around Australia in winter. **HABITS AND HABITAT** While feeding chicks, adults will forage up to 250km offshore for fish, krill and crustaceans. Call a scratchy, chattering sound. **CONSERVATION** Endemic/Nationally Vulnerable. Fledglings hindered by artificial lights and often crash-land onto roads.

Little Shearwater ■ *Puffinus assimilis* 25–28cm; WS 58–67cm
(totorore)

DESCRIPTION ssp. *assimilis* (Norfolk Island), *haurakiensis* (North Island), *kermadecensis* (Kermadec). Small, compact seabird, black above and white below. Grey mottling on sides and face varies between subspecies, but generally pale around eye. Short bill grey tipped black; feet blue with pink webbing. Short, rounded wings and stubby tail. Flies close to the water's surface. **DISTRIBUTION** Breeding islands scattered in outer Hauraki Gulf, Bay of Plenty and Kermadec Islands. Regular in NI waters. **HABITS AND HABITAT** Winter breeder, with eggs laid around July. Wary and usually solitary at sea. Rarely close inshore favouring temperate to tropical waters. Call a series of throaty chatters and 'honks'. **CONSERVATION** Native/ Recovering.

Subantarctic Shearwater ■ *Puffinus elegans* 30cm; WS 58–65cm

DESCRIPTION Very similar to the Little Shearwater (above), but shorter winged with more robust bill, and with more extensive dark feathering on face forming pale eye-ring. Historically treated as single species. **DISTRIBUTION** Majority of birds breed at Antipodes Islands, as well as Star Keys in Chathams. Can be seen at sea throughout subantarctic and occasionally off lower SI. Also in S Atlantic. **HABITS AND HABITAT** Nesting takes place in spring and summer. Eggs laid in short burrows (less than 1m) in August–October, and young fledge as early as December. Forages at sea individually or in loose flocks of several hundred birds. Main predator is the Brown Skua (p. 60). **CONSERVATION** Native/Naturally Uncommon.

Australasian Gannet ■ *Morus serrator* 84–90cm; WS 170–200cm
(tākapu)

DESCRIPTION Large, long-necked seabird. Adult plumage mainly white, apart from yellow wash over head. Pointed wings white with black flight feathers, and tail mostly black. Iris greyish surrounded by a blue eye-ring, and wedge-shaped bill pale grey. Black facial skin borders eye and bill-base. Webbed feet black with green lines running down

toes. Chicks develop white down shortly after hatching. Dark-billed juveniles have brown spotting on head and upperparts. Immatures whiten with age, gaining full adult plumage after three years. South African vagrant **Cape Gannet** M. *capensis* very difficult to distinguish, only two (long-staying) records. **DISTRIBUTION** Three major colonies on mainland: Muriwai in W Auckland, Cape Kidnappers in Hawke's Bay and Farewell Spit in Tasman. Readily seen along NZ coastline, but often in greater numbers further N. Also breeds around SE Australia. **HABITS AND HABITAT** Nesting period August–March, in dense colonies on offshore

Immature

islands, rock stacks, beaches and headlands. Generally forms long-term pair bonds. Single egg laid in compact mound. Neighbouring birds that approach too close likely to witness an aggressive territorial display, or even fall victim to a ruthless attack. Air sacs below skin in face and chest, combined with nictitating eye membrane, protect from injury while plunging from heights of up to 20m. Schools of fish can attract hundreds of individuals in a spectacular dive display. **CONSERVATION** Native/Not Threatened.

Adult with chick

Masked Booby ■ *Sula dactylatra* 75–85cm; WS 160–170cm

DESCRIPTION ssp. *tasmani* (Tasman). Large tropical seabird. Adults completely white, apart from black trailing edge to long wings, and black tail. Wedge-shaped bill lemon-yellow with dark iris and navy blue facial skin. Webbed feet olive to grey in colour. Female has duller bill, and immatures brown on head and upperparts. **DISTRIBUTION** About 100 pairs breed on Kermadec Islands; rarely seen around mainland NZ. Present throughout tropical regions worldwide. **HABITS AND HABITAT** Nests constructed in wind-exposed areas to allow for easy take-offs. Main calls a snappy *kek* and prolonged whistle. **CONSERVATION** Native/Nationally Endangered. Population decline observed after severe El Niño events.

Brown Booby ■ *Sula leucogaster* 65–75cm; WS 130–150cm

DESCRIPTION ssp. *plotus*. Large, chocolate-brown seabird with pointed tail. Adults have white underparts including underwing, with cleanly demarcated breast. Male has blue facial skin; yellow in larger female. Eye and bill pale. Feet light green. Immatures duller around face, with brown mottling (not white) below and light orange feet. **DISTRIBUTION** Straggles to N NZ, near annually at Muriwai in Auckland. Breeds in tropical Pacific, Atlantic and Indian Oceans. **HABITS AND HABITAT** Strongly pelagic. Usually catches fish by plunge diving into the water at a shallow angle. Associates with Australasian Gannets (opposite) while local. Shows no grace at colonies with take-offs and landings, and also give creaky 'honk' call. **CONSERVATION** Native/Vagrant.

Immature female

Great Frigatebird ■ *Fregata minor* 85–105cm; WS 205–230cm

DESCRIPTION Enormous dark seabird with distinctive crooked, narrow wings and long, forked tail. Adult male glossy black with inflatable red throat-pouch. Long, hooked bill grey on male, and pale on female, which also has brown carpal bars, grey throat and white breast. Juveniles have orange heads and white underparts. **DISTRIBUTION** Visitor to Kermadec Islands, with flock of 50 seen in 2021. Very rarely reaches mainland, often following tropical storms. Throughout tropics worldwide. **HABITS AND HABITAT** Strongly pelagic, avoiding land outside breeding season. Targets flying fish and harasses seabirds for their catch; feeds only in flight. **CONSERVATION** Native/Vagrant. **Lesser Frigatebird** *F. ariel* a rare vagrant to NZ.

Male

Female

Pitt Island Shag ■ *Phalacrocorax featherstoni* 63cm ⓔ
(kawau o Rangihaute)

DESCRIPTION Yellow-footed shag. Breeding adults gain forwards-facing crest, lime green facial skin, filoplumes and bluish-black plumage on head, neck, back and tail. Wings mid-grey, each feather tipped in black. Underside pale grey. Brownish bill long and slender. Duller non-breeders lose crest and gain yellow facial skin. **DISTRIBUTION** Restricted to Rekohu/Chatham and Pitt Islands, as well as adjacent islands and islets. **HABITS AND HABITAT** Nests mainly on rocky cliff faces. Forages singly for fish in coastal waters; some birds in parts of brackish Te Whanga Lagoon. Call a series of low, raspy 'honks'. **CONSERVATION** Endemic/Nationally Vulnerable. Roughly 700 pairs, at risk from colony disturbance, predation and fisheries bycatch.

Non-breeding adult

Breeding adult

Spotted Shag ▪ *Phalacrocorax punctatus* 64–74cm ⓔ
(kawau tikitiki)

DESCRIPTION Slender, yellow-footed shag with striking breeding plumage. Double, forwards-facing crest, bluish-green facial skin, and white filoplumes along head, neck and back. Plumage bluish-black on head, neck, back and tail, with broad white stripe running down each side of face. Wings grey, each feather tipped with black spot. Breast and belly pale grey. Cream-coloured bill long and slender with hook at tip. Non-breeders lose head-crest and gain yellow facial skin, with duller overall plumage. Immature birds are plain grey overall with pale underside.
DISTRIBUTION NI population now reduced to lower Hauraki Gulf and around Wellington. Widespread around SI and Rakiura/Stewart Island coastline; strongholds are Marlborough Sounds, Banks Peninsula and Otago coast. **HABITS AND HABITAT** Denizen of rocky shoreline; breeding areas tend to be inaccessible cliff faces and islets. Feeds on small fish, caught up to 16km offshore. Birds often have small stones in their gizzard known as 'rangle' to help grind food or perhaps discourage gut parasites. Call a series of low, raspy 'honks'. **CONSERVATION** Endemic/Nationally Vulnerable. Population has shown marked decline in recent decades due to illegal shooting and drowning in fishing nets; particularly in Hauraki Gulf.

Breeding adult

Juvenile

Non-breeding adult

Little Shag ■ *Microcarbo melanoleucos* 55–65cm
(kawaupaka, Little Pied Cormorant)

DESCRIPTION ssp. *brevirostris*. Small, long-tailed cormorant with a diagnostic stubby yellow bill and black feet. Adults have three distinct morphs. 'White-throated' is completely black apart from white face. 'Intermediate' has smudgy black and white mottling on the underparts. 'Pied' is clean white on the face, throat, breast, belly and vent. All morphs develop a crest while breeding. Some birds may also have orange feathers instead of white from iron-staining. Juveniles are black overall, except pied morphs. **DISTRIBUTION** Common across NZ, Australia, New Guinea and Indonesia.

HABITS AND HABITAT Always in proximity to either freshwater or coastal environments. Forages individually along sea or lake floor for small fish, crustaceans and insects. Generally silent except at colonies. **CONSERVATION** Native/Relict.

Non-breeding pied morph   *Immature*

Pied Shag ■ *Phalacrocorax varius* 65–85cm
(kāruhiruhi, Pied Cormorant)

DESCRIPTION ssp. *varius*. Large cormorant (known locally as shags). Adults clean black and white with yellow facial skin, green iris and blue eye-ring. Hooked bill greyish-pink, brighter during breeding. Webbed feet black. Juveniles lack colours on face, with smudgier plumage and often mottled underparts. **DISTRIBUTION** Common around NZ coast and selected inland sites. Also widespread in Australia. **HABITS AND HABITAT** Forages inshore, in estuaries, harbours and lakes. Mainly feeds on large fish, eels and crustaceans, diving for about 40 seconds in pursuit. Afterwards perches in familiar 'wings-up' pose. Nest constructed in large trees on coastal cliffs. Colony calls reminiscent of manic screams and guttural croaking. **CONSERVATION** Native/Recovering.

Juvenile   *Breeding adult*

Little Black Shag ■ *Phalacrocorax sulcirostris* 60–65cm
(kawau tūī, Little Black Cormorant)

DESCRIPTION Slender, black-footed cormorant. Glossy black; back feathers slate-grey with black outlines. Iris emerald-green. Long, narrow bill purplish-grey, matching facial skin. Breeding birds develop white plumes and filoplumes over neck and subtle bronze tinge. Non-breeding and immature birds have duller brownish plumage. Strong flier, travelling in 'V' formation. **DISTRIBUTION** Fairly widespread across NI and upper SI, spreading southwards. Elsewhere found in Australia, New Guinea and Indonesia. **HABITS AND HABITAT** Nests in typically inland colonies, dispersing afterwards in autumn. Highly gregarious, foraging cooperatively in large flocks of often up to 100 birds, mainly in search of fish. Mostly silent but males utter weak croaks while breeding. **CONSERVATION** Native/Naturally Uncommon.

Black Shag ■ *Phalacrocorax carbo* 80–88cm
(māpunga, Great Cormorant)

DESCRIPTION ssp. *novaehollandiae*. Huge, black-footed cormorant. Mostly black plumage. Eye turquoise and hooked bill grey. Breeding birds gain white face- and flank-patches, plus small crest and white filoplumes. Orange-yellow facial skin at bill-base also more prominent. Non-breeding and immature birds duller brown, the latter with pale blotching over breast. **DISTRIBUTION** Resident across NI, SI, Stewart and Chatham Islands. Found almost worldwide. **HABITS AND HABITAT** Indifferent to habitat as long as there is water nearby. Tackles a variety of shallow aquatic prey including fish, eels and ducklings. Call a staccato braying. **CONSERVATION** Native/Naturally Uncommon. Historically shot by fishermen to reduce competition.

Breeding adult

Non-breeding adult

New Zealand King Shag ■ *Leucocarbo carunculatus* 76cm ⓔ
(kawau pāteketeke)

DESCRIPTION Large, black and white, 'pink-footed' marine shag. Glossy black plumage across head, back and wings, with faint green sheen. Throat and underparts white, as well as wing-patches and scapulars on back. Bill grey to brown. Breeding birds develop prominent yellow caruncles above bill-base, black facial skin and cobalt-blue eye-ring. Unlike other shags in this genus, does not gain noticeable crest. Juveniles have duller brownish plumage, and pale bills and facial skin. **DISTRIBUTION** Range limited to D'Urville Island and outer Marlborough Sounds in upper SI. Key sites are Rahuinui

Island, Duffers Reef, Trio Islands, Sentinel Rock and White Rocks. Rare straggler to Wellington, Tasman and Kaikoura. **HABITS AND HABITAT** Breeding starts in winter in dense colonies on bare slopes and rock stacks, with 1–3 eggs laid in guano-based nest of dried vegetation. Birds capable of deep diving up to 50m in search of wide range of fish species. Call a gull-like cry interspersed with grunts and wheezes. **CONSERVATION** Endemic/ Nationally Endangered. Increasingly threatened by human disturbance, degradation of feeding environment, storm events and use of set nets. Localized population puts species at significant risk from potential single impactful event.

Adults

Otago Shag ■ *Leucocarbo chalconotus* 70cm ⓔ
(matapo)

DESCRIPTION Pink-footed marine shag with dimorphic plumage. Pied morph (20–30 per cent of birds) glossy black above and white below plus wing-panels. Bronze morph entirely glossy black. Bill dark brown; facial skin black. Breeding birds gain crest, small orange caruncles on forehead, red gular pouch at bill-base and blue eye-ring. **DISTRIBUTION** Otago coast from Oamaru down to Catlins. Key sites Oamaru Wharf and Taiaroa Head. Straggles to Canterbury, but occurred as far N as Marlborough before human arrival. **HABITS AND HABITAT** Breeds May–September in dense colonies. Lays 1–3 eggs into raised cup nest built up from plant material and guano. **CONSERVATION** Endemic/ Recovering.

Breeding bronze (left) and pied morphs

Foveaux Shag ■ *Leucocarbo stewarti* 68cm ⓔ
(mapo)

DESCRIPTION Split in 2016 from closely related Otago Shag (above) yet only identifiable by location. Pied birds (50–60 per cent) black and white; bronze birds completely glossy black. Morphs breed together. Bill and iris dull brown; facial skin black; webbed feet pink. Breeding birds gain forwards-facing crest, small, dark orange papillae on face, red gular pouch at bill-base and blue eye-ring. Juveniles have duller brownish plumage. **DISTRIBUTION** Southland endemic found along coast from Bluff to Fiordland, throughout Foveaux Strait and along coast of Rakiura/Stewart Island. **HABITS AND HABITAT** Breeds September onwards on fairly inaccessible islands and islets. Forages in coastal waters generally to 30m deep. **CONSERVATION** Endemic/Nationally Vulnerable.

Chatham Island Shag ■ *Leucocarbo onslowi* 63cm ⓔ
(papua)

DESCRIPTION Marine shag. Glossy black across head, back and wings with faint green sheen; throat, wing-patches and underparts white. Bill greyish, iris brown and feet pink. Breeding birds gain small crest, pronounced orange caruncles and red gular pouch at bill-base, and blue eye-ring. Juveniles have dull brown plumage above and paler bills.

DISTRIBUTION About 12 colonies along coast of Rēkohu/Chatham Island, Pitt Island, Star Keys and islets. **HABITS AND HABITAT** Nests in dense colonies on bare headlands and rock faces. Call a series of guttural 'honks'. **CONSERVATION** Endemic/Nationally Vulnerable, with around 800 breeding pairs. Threatened by disturbance from pigs and weka, overfishing and bycatch.

Bounty Island Shag ■ *Leucocarbo ranfurlyi* 71cm ⓔ

DESCRIPTION Glossy black plumage across head, back and wings. Throat and underparts white, as well as the bold wing-bar. Bill brown-black, iris dark and feet pink. Rounded facial skin dark red, more pronounced during breeding season, with adult birds also gaining impressive crest during this time. **DISTRIBUTION** Breeds only on isolated Bounty Islands in NZ subantarctic. Vagrant to Antipodes Island. **HABITS AND HABITAT** Colonies

confined to inaccessible cliff faces. 'Barking' call of male only heard during mating displays; includes moves such as 'gargling', where head is swung back. **CONSERVATION** Endemic/Naturally Uncommon. Population thought to be stable, with 200–300 pairs. Competes for space with albatrosses, penguins and seals.

Auckland Island Shag

■ *Leucocarbo colensoi* 63cm ⓔ
(kawau o Motu Maha)

DESCRIPTION Sleek marine shag. Glossy greenish-black upperparts and sometimes also throat. Chin and underparts white, and bold wing-bar. Bill greyish-black and feet pink. Breeding birds gain forwards-facing head-crest, elongated yellow caruncles at bill-base, reddish gular pouch and facial skin, and vivid purple eye-ring. Juveniles have duller brownish plumage and paler bills. **DISTRIBUTION** Breeds only on Auckland Islands in NZ subantarctic. Vagrant to Tini Heke/The Snares. **HABITS AND HABITAT** Diet of small fish, marine snails and sea urchins, mostly collected from sea floor. Call within pairs a low purring or ticking, combined with elaborate display when breeding. **CONSERVATION** Endemic/Nationally Vulnerable.

Campbell Island Shag

■ *Leucocarbo campbelli* 63cm ⓔ

DESCRIPTION Pink-footed marine shag. Greenish-black across head, neck, back and wings. Chin and underparts white, as well as the bold wing-bar. Bill purplish-black, iris dark. Breeding birds gain small head-crest and red gular pouch with yellow streak at bill-base. Juveniles have duller brownish plumage and paler bills. **DISTRIBUTION** Breeds only at Campbell Islands in NZ subantarctic. Vagrant to Antipodes Island. **HABITS AND HABITAT** Large colonies found on sheer cliff faces as well as in sea caves. Call a low, nasal 'honk'. **CONSERVATION** Endemic/Naturally Uncommon. Restricted range makes species susceptible to events such as diseases or mammalian predator incursions.

Adult (left) and immature

Kōtuku ◾ *Ardea alba* 83–103cm
(White Heron, Great Egret)

DESCRIPTION ssp. *modesta* (Eastern).Large, slender heron with clean white plumage. Breeding adults have long, pointed black bill, turquoise facial skin, long plumes and long reddish legs. Non-breeders have orange bill, yellow facial skin, no plumes and black legs. Eye yellow to brown; gape extends well past eye unlike rare Australian vagrant **Plumed Egret** *A. intermedia*, which is also smaller with shorter neck. Sexes alike. Appears hunched over while roosting, but neck can extend to 1.5 times body length. Flies slowly with neck retracted. **DISTRIBUTION** Breeds only on Waitangiroto River near Okarito Lagoon in NZ. Migrates all across the country for winter. Also found from Australia as far as India and Japan, with other subspecies found worldwide. **HABITS AND HABITAT** Birds start to arrive at colony in August, where nests are built from dry branches and twigs in trees to 15m high over water. Clutch size 3–5 pale green eggs, incubated by both parents. Chicks fed regurgitated fish including whitebait, and leave nest about 64 days after hatching. Frogs, skinks and small birds also taken by adults while foraging, by waiting motionless for prey to pass. Outside breeding season, birds frequent harbours and estuaries, and sometimes freshwater wetlands. Call a harsh croak generally only heard in colony. **CONSERVATION** Native/Nationally Critical. Stable population of about 200 birds, but abundant overseas.

Breeding adult

Non-breeding adult

Cattle Egret ■ *Bubulcus ibis* 46–56cm

DESCRIPTION ssp. *coromandus* (Eastern). Small egret. All white with orange-yellow bill and facial skin, yellow eye and dark legs. Breeding plumage provides plumes on neck and back, and orange wash over head and breast. Facial skin, bill and legs gain reddish flush. **DISTRIBUTION** First recorded in 1963; small flocks migrate regularly from Australia over winter. Reliable sites include Kaipara Harbour and Lake Ellesmere. Widespread across SE Asia and Oceania. **HABITS AND HABITAT** Forages in rural areas close to livestock, which tends to disturb prey. Favours invertebrates such as crickets and earthworms. Silent apart from various croaks and chatters while breeding, not yet confirmed in NZ. **CONSERVATION** Native/ Not Threatened.

Breeding adult

Non-breeding adult

Little Egret
■ *Egretta garzetta* 55–65cm

DESCRIPTION ssp. *immaculata*. Small, pure white heron with long bill, and yellow facial skin and iris. Lower mandible of black bill yellowish. Long legs and feet dull yellow to black. In breeding plumage birds gain two plumes behind head, as well as on breast and back, and facial skin can flush red. **DISTRIBUTION** Near-annual visitor to NZ, usually single birds to same site, such as Manawatū Estuary. Widespread across Australasia, Europe and Africa. **HABITS AND HABITAT** Often observed at coastal sites, lagoons and estuaries, but will also visit freshwater ponds and wetlands. Feeding style can involve stealth to ambush small fish and invertebrates. Call a quavering croak. **CONSERVATION** Native/Vagrant.

Non-breeding adult

White-faced Heron ■ *Egretta novaehollandiae* 60–70cm
(matuku moana)

Juvenile

DESCRIPTION ssp. *novaehollandiae*. Slender, medium-sized heron. Blue-grey (paler below); white face and throat diagnostic. Pointed bill, facial skin and flight feathers dark grey; breast has russet tinge. Plumes on breast and back longer in breeding plumage. Flies with tucked back head and trailing yellow legs. Immature birds have reduced white on face. **DISTRIBUTION** Became established in 1940s after self-introduction from Australia; now common and widespread over NZ. **HABITS AND HABITAT** Present in range of environments: rocky shores, estuaries, lakes and wetlands, damp pasture and urban parks. Often seen walking slowly out in the open foraging for prey. Harsh, guttural croak often heard during flight, or aggressive interactions. **CONSERVATION** Native/Not Threatened.

Breeding adult

Reef Heron ■ *Egretta sacra* 58–66cm
(matuku moana, Eastern Reef Egret)

DESCRIPTION ssp. *sacra*. Slate-grey egret with heavy bill varying in colour from orange to black, and greenish yellow legs. Iris yellow; some birds have white streak on chin. Develops plumes on head and breast during breeding. Pure white morph found overseas, recorded once in NZ. Juveniles grey-brown. **DISTRIBUTION** Scarce around NZ coast and islands, more common in NI. Also found across Oceania and SE Asia. **HABITS AND HABITAT** Solitary; territories of adjacent pairs often many kilometres apart. Mainly lives on rocky shores, where plumage provides effective camouflage. Crouches in water with outstretched wings to entice prey close to be stabbed and consumed. Call a nasal *kraak*. **CONSERVATION** Native/Nationally Endangered, with 300–500 estimated. Abundant in rest of range.

Adult

Nankeen Night Heron ■ *Nycticorax caledonicus* 55–65cm
(Rufous Night Heron, umu kōtuku)

DESCRIPTION ssp. *australasiae*. Stocky rufous heron with dark cap. Greenish lores with yellow eye; dark bill long and tapered. Pale below with yellow legs. Breeding birds have white plume extending from head. Juveniles heavily streaked in brown and buff tones. **DISTRIBUTION** Self-introduced from Australia in 1950s; only known to breed along Whanganui River and side streams in C NI. Vagrants occasionally appear elsewhere in NZ. **HABITS AND HABITAT** Nocturnal and rarely seen. By day birds concealed in thick vegetation, but will sun themselves on edges of roost trees. Forages at night for fish and invertebrates along water courses. Call a series of high-pitched croaks. **CONSERVATION** Native/Colonizer.

Juvenile   *Adult*

Australasian Bittern ■ *Botaurus poiciloptilus* 65–75cm
(matuku-hūrepo)

DESCRIPTION Bulky, dinosaur-like heron with intricate brown and buff patterning on back and wings. Plumage variable, though in all cases pale from throat down to breast and belly, marked with dark blotches. Head chocolate-brown with white patch above eye, buff across cheeks, and lores blue to greenish-grey. Sharp bill beige, darker on upper mandible. Juveniles lighter overall, with yellow irises turning ochre with age. In flight dull green legs trail behind creating distinctive silhouette, along with folded up neck and broad, slow-moving wings. **DISTRIBUTION** Widespread across NZ though very scarce; bulk of population in upper NI. Also resident in Australia. **HABITS AND HABITAT** Bitterns live almost exclusively in freshwater areas – lake and river verges, reed beds, peat bogs and even flooded paddocks. Research indicates that they migrate away from breeding grounds during winter. Tends to be incredibly wary – in response to threats, stands upright and freezes, skulks beneath vegetation or inelegantly flushes into the air. Takes fish, eels, frogs and occasionally small mammals as prey. In spring and summer, territorial males perform to attract females. Usually heard before dawn and after dusk. Inflates throat to produce resonating 'boom' that can be heard for up to 2km. Also makes *kraak* call between individuals. **CONSERVATION** Native/Nationally Critical, with less than 1,000 birds thought to remain. Threatened by several factors, notably drainage of wetlands that causes habitat loss and decline in food supply.

Glossy Ibis ▪ *Plegadis falcinellus* 48–66cm

DESCRIPTION Large wading bird with long, downcurved bill. Adults appear dark from afar, but sport striking multicoloured iridescent plumage. Crimson overall, darker purple on back and green-bronze wings. Long brown legs. Non-breeding and juvenile birds duller, with faint pale flecking over head and neck. Flies with neck outstretched. **DISTRIBUTION** Vagrants regularly show up over most of NZ. Several pairs have bred at Wairau Lagoons, Marlborough, every summer since 2015, with a high count of 23 birds reported. Appears to be slowly increasing in numbers. Cosmopolitan; widespread throughout warmer regions globally. **HABITS AND HABITAT** Sightings occur in freshwater wetlands, damp pasture and estuaries. Specialized sickle-shaped bill facilitates probing for invertebrates. Call a raspy croak, seldom heard. **CONSERVATION** Native/Colonizer.

Breeding adult

Non-breeding adult

Royal Spoonbill ▪ *Platalea regia* 74–81cm
(kōtuku ngutupapa)

DESCRIPTION Bizarre bald-faced white waterbird with black spoon-shaped bill and long black legs. Breeding adults have buff breast, yellow patches above each eye and red spot on forehead. Long crest feathers on back of head to 20cm long on males. Smaller juveniles lack facial colouring and head-crest entirely. Flies with neck outstretched and legs trailing behind. **DISTRIBUTION** Self-introduced in 1949; now common and still increasing across mainland NZ. Widespread in Australia. **HABITS AND HABITAT** Breeds coastally, dispersing to freshwater wetlands and tidal estuaries in winter. Walks slowly through water, sweeping peculiar bill from side to side, catching mainly fish and crustaceans. Call a low, guttural *caw*. **CONSERVATION** Native/Naturally Uncommon.

Immature

Breeding adult

Black Kite ▪ *Milvus migrans* 45–55cm; WS 140–150cm

DESCRIPTION ssp. *affinis*. Mid-sized hawk with long, forked tail. Adults rich brown with dark eye-patch and buff shoulders. Hooked bill black with yellow cere, and legs. Pale circle on underside of dark wings; primaries long and reaching. Rectangular wings held horizontally in flight; often gliding and soaring. **DISTRIBUTION** Rare visitor to NZ (including long-staying bird near Renwick, Marlborough, from 1992 to 2019). Occurs widely across Africa, Eurasia and Australia. **HABITS AND HABITAT** Favours open plains and rural areas. Opportunistic, feeding on carrion, but also hunts small animals. Call a shrill, quavering *kwee-e-e*. **CONSERVATION** Native/Vagrant.

Swamp Harrier ▪ *Circus approximans* 50–58cm; WS 120–145cm
(kāhu, Australasian Harrier)

DESCRIPTION Large raptor. Adults tawny-brown with clear facial discs, barred underwings and pale streaked belly. Juveniles entirely chocolate-brown, including eye. Lightens with successive moults. Strongly hooked bill highlighted by yellow cere, and rufous feathering on thighs; long yellow legs and taloned feet. Broad wings form 'V' shape with fingered primaries. White rump evident in flight. **DISTRIBUTION**

Widespread across mainland NZ and Chatham Islands, as well as Australia and W Pacific. **HABITS AND HABITAT** Familiar sight in rural areas, gliding on thermals or perched on roadsides. Nests mainly at ground level in dense vegetation. Opportunistic, feeding on carrion but also hunting birds and mammals. Call a sharp *kek* or *kee-o*. **CONSERVATION** Native/ Not Threatened.

Adult   *Immature*

New Zealand Falcon ■ *Falco novaeseelandiae* 40–50cm; WS 63–98cm ⓔ
(kārearea)

DESCRIPTION Robust, medium-sized raptor with short, broad, pointed wings. Adults dark grey-brown above with pale throat and underside, the latter also streaked brown. Wings and long tail neatly barred with light brown, more intensely underneath. Shaggy orange 'trousers' sit above long yellow legs and fine black claws. Yellow facial skin, eye-ring and base of hooked black bill. Female about 65 per cent heavier than male. Juveniles much darker on breast and belly, with greyish face and legs instead of yellow. Australian vagrant **Nankeen Kestrel** *F. cenchroides* smaller and more delicate with mainly rufous colouring, and preference for hover hunting. **DISTRIBUTION** Widespread but sparse across mainland NZ; rarely seen N of Waikato. Also resident on subantarctic Auckland Islands. **HABITS AND HABITAT** Versatile, occurring in mature native and exotic forests as well as tussock grassland and rough open country. Some birds have home ranges that also encompass urban areas. In spring, lays up to four rusty-brown eggs in nest scrape, often at ground level. Eggs fiercely defended by dive bombing any potential threats, including humans. Once chicks fledge, dispersing juveniles can turn up anywhere. Impressive high-speed hunter, preying on birds, mammals and insects on the wing. Call a piercing, repetitive *kek-kek-kek-kek*. **CONSERVATION** Endemic/Recovering. Loss of suitable breeding sites from habitat modification and clearance. Electrocution also an ongoing threat. Population estimated at 6,000–8,000 birds.

Female

Juvenile

Adult male

Ruru ▪ *Ninox novaseelandiae* 26–29cm
(Morepork)

DESCRIPTION ssp. *novaseelandiae*. Small, compact owl with dark russet-brown plumage, prominent pale cream streaking on underside and bright yellow eyes set in dark facial mask. Small bill grey-green, and amount of white on face varies. Feathers continue down

to feet, which are yellow with fine black claws. Juveniles smaller and greyer, retaining some of chick down. Flight silent, resulting from soft, bristle-like edges to brown- and white-blotched flight feathers. **DISTRIBUTION** Widely distributed across mainland NZ and close surrounding islands with sufficient tree cover; less common in drier parts of eastern SI. Other subspecies occurs in Tasmania, Australia and Norfolk Island (hybridized with NZ subspecies after being introduced to save the population). **HABITS AND HABITAT** Nocturnal, roosting by day in shaded vegetation in forests, and well-vegetated parks and gardens. Tree cavities are preferred nesting sites. Occasionally active at dawn or dusk; best viewed around outdoor light sources hunting moths attracted to the light. Diet predominantly insects, mice and small birds; prey seized from overlooking perches. Known by distinctive *morepork* or *ruru* call, for which it is named. **CONSERVATION** Native/Not Threatened. Common across NZ but still susceptible to predation from introduced mammalian predators such as cats and stoats.

Juvenile

Adult

Adult

Little Owl ▪ *Athene noctua* 21–23cm
(ruru nohinohi)

DESCRIPTION Very small owl with pale eyes
and white brow. Warm-grey plumage above
with bold white spotting, and white underparts
strongly streaked grey. Wing feathers and
short tail light brown with buff blotches.
Hooked bill dull yellow. Bobs up and down
when alarmed. **DISTRIBUTION** Introduced
from Germany in 1906; fairly common in
SI from Nelson and Marlborough down E
coast to Southland. Found naturally across
Eurasia. **HABITS AND HABITAT** Most
active at dawn and dusk but can be observed
by day in well-vegetated parks and rural areas.
Nests in man-made structures, wood piles
or tree holes. Rodents and insects make up
most of diet. Main call a high-pitched *kiew*.
CONSERVATION Introduced and naturalized.

Barn Owl ▪ *Tyto alba* 33–38cm

DESCRIPTION ssp. *delicatula* (Australian).
Ghostly, medium-sized owl. Dark eyes and
hooked pink bill encircled by pale, heart-
shaped face. Golden-brown head, back and
upperwings accented by intricately patterned,
mottled grey feathers. White underparts can
have light speckling. Feathers continue down
to pinkish feet. **DISTRIBUTION** Release
in Auckland in 1990s failed but then self-
introduced from Australia; first recorded
breeding near Kaitaia, Northland, in 2008.
Rare visitor to rest of NZ. Widespread
from S Asia to Pacific. **HABITS AND
HABITAT** Favours rural areas, farmland and
open woodland. Nests made in tree holes
high above the ground. Feeds mainly on
rodents and small birds, hovering over fields
momentarily before pouncing. Call a harsh,
rising screech. **CONSERVATION** Native/
Colonizer. Potential threat to other native
species in NZ; yet to be studied in detail.

Sacred Kingfisher ■ *Todiramphus sanctus* 21–23cm
(kōtare)

DESCRIPTION ssp. *vagans* (New Zealand). Small kingfisher with bright blue on crown, upperwings and tail. Upper back and forehead dull green. Eye-stripe black, as well as tips of primaries and tail. Underparts orange to buff, fading with wear. Broad collar goes around neck, and small patch in front of brown eye. White crescent beneath eye. Heavy black bill with pinkish base to lower mandible. Female tends to have smaller pale patch above eye, lighter belly and less vivid colouring. Immatures have pale scalloping on crown and shoulders, and brown mottling across chest. Fast flying with short glides between wingbeats. **DISTRIBUTION** Common resident on NI, SI and Rakiura/Stewart Islands, close offshore islands and Kermadec Islands. Also occurs across Australia, New Caledonia, New Guinea and Indonesia. **HABITS AND HABITAT** Found readily in range of environments: coastal mudflats, rocky shores, freshwater lakes and wetlands, as well as open country, parks, gardens and native forest. Partially migratory, moves nearer to coast during winter. Female lays

4–7 eggs in tree hole or clay bank burrow. Perches characteristically in the open while searching for food. Small fish, reptiles and invertebrates preferred, but small birds and mammals sometimes fall prey. Main call a loud *ek-ek-ek-ek* repeated in succession. Also an ascending *crew-crew* when birds meet and various screeches of alarm. **CONSERVATION** Native/Not Threatened.

Adult

Immature

Laughing Kookaburra ■ *Dacelo novaeguineae* 40–45cm

DESCRIPTION ssp. *novaeguineae*. Large, bulky kingfisher. Cream undersides and head with brown blotches on crown and cheek behind eye. Back and wings chocolate-brown; wing-coverts pale blue. Tail feathers barred orange and black. Enormous bill grey and beige; legs dull yellow. Male distinguished by blue wash on flight feathers and rump.

DISTRIBUTION Introduced from E Australia to Kawau Island, Auckland, in 1860s. Now found in low numbers to N and W of Auckland, and may still be spreading. **HABITS AND HABITAT** Occupies exotic pine plantations, open woodland and farmland. Often seen perched on power lines surveying for reptile and invertebrate prey. Known for very distinctive, laughing call. **CONSERVATION** Introduced and naturalized.

White-throated Needletail ■ *Hirundapus caudacutus* 20cm; WS 49cm
(Spine-tailed Swift)

DESCRIPTION ssp. *caudacutus*. Torpedo-shaped bird with long, pointed wings; can spend years in flight without landing. Large black eye, and stubby bill and legs. Plumage dark brown with white throat-patch, and another below tail. Centre of back pale grey; wings and tail black with blue sheen. Needle-like projections on tail feathers visible up close. **DISTRIBUTION** Not resident. Single birds regularly blown over from Australia, with rare invasions reported of up to hundreds at a time. **HABITS AND HABITAT** One of the fastest flying birds, with reported speeds of up to 169kph. Forages for insects exclusively in flight; often on verge of low-pressure systems. Call a rapid chattering. **CONSERVATION** Native/Vagrant. Darker **Fork-tailed Swift** *Apus pacificus* visits even less frequently.

Kākāpō ■ *Strigops habroptila* 58–64cm ⓔ

DESCRIPTION Huge, flightless parrot; green morph has mossy-green plumage with dark markings on upper feathers. Face and underside more yellow, with less intense markings. Olive morph is dull yellow overall. Wings short and rounded. Primary and tail feathers pale yellow with black barring. Buff bristles on face extend from behind black eye over cheek to above prominent nostrils. Pale grey bill hooks down from face. Feathers continue down to large grey feet. Chicks coated in grey downy feathers. **DISTRIBUTION** Extinct across former mainland range; isolated populations now exist, the largest on Whenua Hou/

Codfish Island and Pukenui/Anchor Islands, while Te Kakahu/Chalky Island in Fiordland and Hauturu/Little Barrier Island near Auckland hold remainder. **HABITS AND HABITAT** Nocturnal, feeding throughout the night in native forest and scrubland. Entirely herbivorous; ground-dwelling but climbs high into podocarp trees to reach berries and leaves. Breeding influenced by abundance of food; only happens every 2–4 years. Being lek breeders, males produce deep 'boom' and *ching* sounds to attract females to their bowl, where they display in an effort to mate. Nests on ground, lays 1–4 white eggs, and feeds chicks for three months after hatching. Lifespan could exceed 90 years. Makes a variety of hoarse *skraark*s and grunting calls. **CONSERVATION** Endemic/Nationally Critical. Extremely common prior to human arrival, now all but wiped out by cats, stoats and rats. Population reached a high of 252 in 2022 (from a low of 51 in the 1990s), there are still many risks such as disease and inbreeding. Kākāpō Recovery Programme closely manages the species conservation.

Green morph

Olive morph

Chicks in nest

Kea ■ *Nestor notabilis* 46–50cm e

DESCRIPTION Large parrot with smart olive-green plumage. Feathers have dark outer edges, giving scaled appearance. Underwings striking reddish-orange, accented by dark flight feathers with pale yellow spots. Upperwings dark green with blue edges on primaries; back green turning reddish on rump. Tail feathers turquoise with dark band near tip. Long grey-black bill strongly hooked downwards, with nostrils that are pale on immature birds. Juveniles told by yellow eye-ring, nostrils and lower mandible of bill. **DISTRIBUTION** Resident mostly at higher altitudes across SI; from Tasman and inland Marlborough down along Southern Alps to Fiordland, as well as Kaikoura Ranges. **HABITS AND HABITAT** Playful and intelligent bird of high country, alpine tussock fields and scree slopes. Breeding rarely occurs below 700m, but they often descend into

Juvenile

native forests after heavy snow events or in search of food. Natural diet mainly consists of leaves, fruits and invertebrates. However, with its opportunistic nature, it has been heavily influenced by humans who donate scraps of food, where their ranges overlap. Māori name was given for its call, best depicted as *kee-ee-aa-aa*. **CONSERVATION** Endemic/Nationally Endangered. Bounty placed on Kea for their sporadic sheep attacks was outlawed in 1971, but still managed to catastrophically reduce the population, with only 4,000–6,000 birds thought to remain. Nests also vulnerable to predation from rats and mustelids.

Adult

Kākā ▪ *Nestor meridionalis* 38–44cm ⓔ

DESCRIPTION ssp. *septentrionalis* (North Island), *meridionalis* (South Island). Medium-sized forest parrot with overall brown colouring and deep red-tipped feathers on nape, belly and rump. Underwings striking reddish-orange, accented by dark flight feathers with pale orange markings. Tail feathers brown above and reddish below, with dark band near tip. SI birds have stronger white cap and greenish tinge to upperparts. Large, slate-grey bill curved downwards, with prominent nostrils that are yellow in juveniles, as well as the eye-ring. Grey feet zygodactyl as in all parrots (two toes face forwards, two backwards). **DISTRIBUTION** Sparse across NI and SI in suitable habitat, but found in good numbers on Aotea/Great Barrier Island and Rakiura/Stewart Island, as well as many offshore islands including Waiheke near Auckland. Reintroduction programmes have proven successful, with birds released at Zealandia Ecosanctuary going on to repopulate greater Wellington area. **HABITS AND HABITAT** Boisterous parrot well known for raucous behaviour in groups, but can be discreet when alone. Favours mature native forests including podocarp and beech, but can show up anywhere while travelling to and from breeding grounds. Nests constructed in tree holes. Diet comprises leaves, fruits and occasionally nectar; also enjoys stripping bark off trees in search of wood-dwelling invertebrates. Boasts impressive repertoire of squawks, shrieks, whistles and clicks, sometimes heard after dark. **CONSERVATION** Endemic/Recovering; population estimated at over 10,000 individuals. Nests and brooding females vulnerable to predation from introduced predators, primarily rats and mustelids.

Adult South Island subspecies

Adult North Island subspecies

Sulphur-crested Cockatoo ■
Cacatua galerita 48–55cm

DESCRIPTION ssp. *galerita*. Familiar large parrot. Entirely white plumage with spectacular yellow crest that can be raised at will. Broad wings and tail have pale yellow wash underneath. Eye black; large, curved bill dark grey, and feet pale grey. **DISTRIBUTION** Populations established from escaped cage birds in Auckland, Waikato, Whanganui and Banks Peninsula. Originates from Australia and New Guinea. **HABITS AND HABITAT** Keeps mainly to rural areas, including lowland hill country, open woodland and native forest. Grain-based diet. Most active at dusk when large flocks form while flying around and calling, then roost together overnight in stands of tall trees. Loud, raucous call sometimes combined with yodelling whistle. **CONSERVATION** Introduced and naturalized.

Galah ■ *Eolophus roseicapillus* 35cm

DESCRIPTION Greyish parrot with bright pink face and underside, and pale cap that raises into short crest. Bill light grey; iris dark in male and orange-red in female. Wings narrow; flight feathers and underside of tail dark grey. Juveniles told by smaller crest and duller plumage.
DISTRIBUTION Small populations established as result of escaped cage birds from 1950s onwards. Key sites are Ponui Island, and Mangatawhiri S of Auckland. Originates from Australia. **HABITS AND HABITAT** Uncommon and possibly declining, with most sightings among fields of maize stubble and surrounding agricultural land. Gregarious, feeding predominately on seeds, crops and grasses. Call a piercing, repetitive *whee-op whee-op*. **CONSERVATION** Introduced and naturalized.

Red-crowned Parakeet ■ *Cyanoramphus novaezelandiae* 25–28cm 🇪
(kākāriki)

DESCRIPTION ssp. *novaezelandiae, cyanurus* (Kermadec), *chathamensis* (Chatham Island). Best known of NZ endemic *cyanoramphus* parakeets. Bright green parrot with small

Adult Chatham Island subspecies

crimson patch on crown continuing to behind eyes, and one on either side of rump. Flight feathers dark, with turquoise-blue highlights varying in hue and intensity between subspecies. Breast and belly more lime-green in colour, and long tail emerald-green. Iris red; bill silver with black tip and cutting edge; zygodactyl feet grey. Female smaller than male, with yellow stripe on underwing seen in flight. Young birds have darker eyes and pinkish bill. **DISTRIBUTION** Ranges N to Kermadecs, E to Chathams and S to Auckland Islands. Mainland sightings rare apart from around reintroduction sites, such as Zealandia Ecosanctuary, Wellington. Flourishing on offshore islands such as in Hauraki Gulf, Three Kings, Kapiti Island and Rakiura/Stewart Island. **HABITS AND HABITAT** Occurs in native forest and shrubland, often near coast. Cavity nester, favouring tree holes, but also utilizes burrows in clay banks or soil, or simply dense vegetation. Omnivorous diet consists mainly of leaves, fruits and flowers. Call a brisk, repetitive chatter that resembles *ter-ter-ter-ter-ter-ter*. **CONSERVATION** Endemic/Relict. Remains threatened by mammalian predators (rats, stoats and cats) and nearly went extinct on mainland, as well as parrot-centric diseases such as Beak and Feather Disease.

Adult mainland subspecies

Yellow-crowned Parakeet

■ *Cyanoramphus auriceps* 23–27cm  (e)
(kākāriki)

DESCRIPTION Bright green parrot with crimson front and yellow forecrown. Flight feathers dark-edged turquoise to blue; long tail emerald-green. Underside more lime-green. Bill silver with black tip; feet grey. **DISTRIBUTION** Sparse across C NI. In SI bulk of birds found in proximity to Southern Alps and Fiordland. More conspicuous on certain offshore islands such as Hauturu/Little Barrier, Mana and Ulva Islands. **HABITS AND HABITAT** Spends most of its time as flocks high in the canopy of mature native forest, in search of fruit, buds and seeds. Generally summer breeder, but nests year round in times of high food abundance. Call a high-pitched, rapid chatter. **CONSERVATION** Endemic/ Declining.

Adult

Orange-fronted Parakeet

■ *Cyanoramphus malherbi* 19–22cm (e)
(kākāriki karaka, Malherbe's Parakeet)

DESCRIPTION Small, spring-green parrot. Diagnostic orange band above bill sits between red eye and pale yellow crown. Outer wing dark with blue highlights; long tail emerald-green. Orange flank-patch above grey legs. Nostrils grey, and bill silver with abrupt black tip. Young birds have pinkish legs. **DISTRIBUTION** Restricted to SI in Hurunui, Poulter and Hawdon Valleys. Translocated to Brook Waimārama Sanctuary in Nelson and offshore islands, notably Blumine Island in Marlborough Sounds. **HABITS AND HABITAT** Requires mature native beech forest. Nest constructed in tree hole. Diet of leaves and berries. Call a sweet, bubbling chatter. **CONSERVATION** Endemic/Nationally Critical. Very vulnerable to introduced predators. Wild populations supplemented by captive breeding. Fewer than 500 remain.

Adult

Forbes' Parakeet ■ *Cyanoramphus forbesi* 28cm ⓔ

DESCRIPTION Medium-sized green parrot with yellow forecrown and red frontal band that does not meet the eye. Face and belly yellowish. Flight feathers turquoise to blue, with

red spot on either side of rump. Underwings and long tail emerald-green. Bill silver with black tip; feet grey. **DISTRIBUTION** Endemic to Rēkohu/Chatham Islands, resident on Māngere and Little Māngere Islands. Visits Pitt Island on occasion. **HABITS AND HABITAT** Mostly stays high in the canopy of mature forest after fruits, buds and seeds. Also scrub and grassland. Call a typical parakeet chatter. **CONSERVATION** Endemic/ Nationally Endangered. At risk from large-scale hybridization with Red-crowned Parakeet, but today hybrids make up less than 10 per cent of birds.

Reischek's Parakeet ■ *Cyanoramphus hochstetteri* 28cm ⓔ

DESCRIPTION Dumpy lime-green parrot with red patches on crown, around eye and on either side of rump. Underwing and pale-edged flight feathers dark blue-green. Bill silver with black tip and cutting edge; feet grey. Juveniles distinguished by shorter tails with pale

feather tips. **DISTRIBUTION** Endemic to Antipodes Island, with smaller numbers also on adjacent islets. **HABITS AND HABITAT** Occurs along rocky coasts, and in tussock grassland and mega-herb fields. Feeds on tussock flowers, leaves, seeds, berries and occasionally invertebrates. Flocks seasonally to food sources. Call a typical chatter. **CONSERVATION** Endemic/Naturally Uncommon. Significant population growth following island-wide rodent eradication in 2016.

Antipodes Island Parakeet ■ *Cyanoramphus unicolor* 29–32cm ⓔ

DESCRIPTION Large, robust green parrot with emerald-green head and tail. Only *Cyanoramphus* species without distinct crown colour. Wing-coverts blue and flight feathers black with blue-green hues. Iris orange; large bill grey with black tip. Male larger than female. **DISTRIBUTION** Endemic to subantarctic Antipodes Island and surrounding islets. **HABITS AND HABITAT** With little in the way of trees or shelter, nests in burrows below the ground. Diet mostly leaves, but also scavenges carrion and eggs, even killing seabirds. Call a low, loud chatter. **CONSERVATION** Endemic/Naturally Uncommon. Increased dramatically after Antipodes declared predator-free, but still at risk from looming chance of incursion.

Eastern Rosella

■ *Platycercus eximius* 30cm
(kākā uhi whero)

DESCRIPTION Brightly coloured parrot with vivid red head and white cheek-patches. Rump and back feathers pale green, latter with large black spots. Underside yellow to green with red vent. Wing-coverts and outer-tail feathers black to pale blue. Primaries and underwing dark blue; blue-green tail long and broad. Bill pale and iris dark brown. Juveniles duller with more widespread green colouring. **DISTRIBUTION** Introduction from SE Australia in 1900, found in Dunedin and across NI (sparse in E and C regions). **HABITS AND HABITAT** Common resident of urban areas and forest margins within its range. Diet dominated by seeds. Notable calls a noisy, rippling chatter, and drawn-out, metallic *ping*. **CONSERVATION** Introduced and naturalized. May compete with kākāriki in areas where they coexist.

Adult

Juvenile

Rifleman ■ *Acanthisitta chloris* 7–9cm (e)
(tītitipounamu)

DESCRIPTION ssp. *granti* (North Island), *chloris* (South Island). NZ's smallest bird. Resembles tiny, beady-eyed ball of feathers with slender, upturned bill and stubby tail. Male lime-green above and whitish below with pale yellow accents. Short, rounded wings dark with green highlights. Face white except for dark patches on either side of eye. Female streaked yellow-brown in lieu of green, and juveniles boldly speckled. **DISTRIBUTION** Patchy across NI; widespread in SI excluding Canterbury and Otago plains. Resident on several islands adjacent to mainland. **HABITS AND HABITAT** Limited to mature native forest. Actively forages for tiny invertebrates in the canopy and along tree trunks. Call exceptionally high-pitched *seep-seep* often accompanied by wing beats not always audible to people. **CONSERVATION** Endemic/Not Threatened.

Male

Female

Rock Wren ■ *Xenicus gilviventris* 10cm (e)
(pīwauwau)

DESCRIPTION One of two surviving members of ancient NZ wren family. Male olive-green above and beige below with yellow flanks. Wings rounded with black outer feathers; tail stubby. Dark brown crown and face divided by pale eyebrow-stripe. Short, straight bill, long legs and pinkish toes. Female similar with sepia colour scheme. Flicks wings and bobs up and down energetically. **DISTRIBUTION** Endemic to SI above 900m altitude. Key sites Arthur's Pass and Homer Tunnel. Translocated to Secretary Island in Fiordland. **HABITS AND HABITAT** Strictly alpine species found among scree slopes and boulder fields with scattered vegetation. Diet of insects, and berries when available. Call a high-pitched *seep-sip-sip*. **CONSERVATION** Endemic/Nationally Endangered.

Male

Female

Grey Warbler ▪ *Gerygone igata* 11cm 🇪
(riroriro, Grey Gerygone)

DESCRIPTION Small, dainty passerine. Pale grey with olive-brown crown, wings and tail (tipped white beneath). Black stripe traverses crimson eye. Tiny bill and thin legs black. Juveniles warmer brown with dark eye. **DISTRIBUTION** Widespread across mainland NZ and inshore islands. **HABITS AND HABITAT** Active bird of vegetated areas including native forest, urban parks and gardens. Insectivorous, foraging on tree trunks and leaves for small spiders, flies, caterpillars and moths. Main host for brood parasite. Shining Cuckoo (p. 31), which often targets second clutch (after migration). Lays 3–5 eggs in unique pear-shaped nest. High-pitched, ringing warble of male most vigorous in spring. **CONSERVATION** Endemic/Not Threatened.

Juvenile

Caption

Chatham Island Warbler ▪ *Gerygone albofrontata* 12cm 🇪
(Chatham Gerygone)

DESCRIPTION Adult male white on face and underside, with warm brown crown and wings. Narrow bill black, and eye red with brown stripe. Tail dark with pale band at each end. Female lacks white forehead and has duller underparts. Juveniles have pink bill, dark eye and yellow wash over face and breast. **DISTRIBUTION** Present across Rēkohu/Chatham Island archipelago, rare in N of main Chatham Island. **HABITS AND HABITAT** Found in native forest; forages in the canopy and at ground level for small invertebrates. Enclosed nest constructed by female, in which 3–4 eggs are laid. Male song a series of 4–5 twittering notes. **CONSERVATION** Endemic/Recovering.

Juvenile

Adult male

Tūi ■ *Prosthemadera novaeseelandiae* 27–32cm ⓔ
(kōkō)

DESCRIPTION ssp. *novaeseelandiae, chathamensis* (Chatham Island). Iconic forest bird that appears black when seen poorly, but bursts into colour when seen well, revealing iridescent turquoise on flight and tail feathers. Head and breast have deep green sheen, and back matte-brown. Wispy white feathers on neck form collar around prominent central tuft. Slightly downcurved bill, long legs and sharp claws jet-black; iris dark brown. Female noticeably smaller than male; juveniles truly black overall, with yellow gape. Chatham subspecies also larger. Flight undulating and flappy. Birds can have orange or purple crowns due to pollen collected from flowers while feeding. **DISTRIBUTION** Common from Kermadec Islands S throughout mainland to Rakiura/Stewart Island, as well as adjacent offshore islands, Auckland Islands; separate subspecies unique to Rēkohu/Chatham Islands. Conspicuously absent from drier parts of Canterbury and Otago. **HABITS AND HABITAT** Widespread in suburban areas; parks, gardens and native forest. Notoriously

aggressive defender of territory and food sources such as flowering pōhutukawa and kōwhai trees, from which it drinks nectar, a major component of its diet. Seasonally feeds on honeydew, fruits and insects. Nest a bulky structure of twigs lined with grass, built by female. Call a varied combination of liquid whistles, guttural croaks, clicks and wheezes (generally harsher than Bellbird's, opposite). **CONSERVATION** Endemic/ Not Threatened.

Adult with pollen crown

Immature

Adult

Bellbird ■ *Anthornis melanura* 17–20cm (e)
(korimako)

DESCRIPTION ssp. *obscura* (Three Kings), *oneho* (Poor Knights), *melanura*. Small, olive-green passerine. Male bright with purple iridescence on face, black lores and deep red iris. Outer-wing and tail feathers black, and vent pale. Slender legs slate-grey and curved bill black. Female more drab overall with subtle green sheen on face, and white stripe just below brown eye. Juveniles greyish with yellow gape. **DISTRIBUTION** Locally common in NI. Sparse N of Waikato; on Hauraki Gulf Islands, in mainland sanctuaries and Hunua Ranges. Common throughout SI, Stewart and Auckland Islands, as well as most inshore islands. **HABITS AND HABITAT** Favours native forest, but will venture into urban areas, especially further S. Also found less often in open woodland and exotic forest. Member of honeyeater family, feeds voraciously on nectar with brush-tipped tongue, from a variety of native and introduced flowering plants. Partial to fruits when in season; during nesting switches to high-protein insect diet to support chick growth. Highly territorial at this time, but otherwise occasionally disperses over long distances. Melodic song performed by puffed up male reminiscent of silver bells and interspersed with the odd croak and wheeze, which varies throughout its range but averages simpler than that of tūī. **CONSERVATION** Endemic/Not Threatened.

Female

Juvenile

Male

North Island Kōkako ■ *Callaeas wilsoni* 38cm ⓔ

DESCRIPTION Large, ghostly member of endemic NZ wattlebird family. Greyish-brown upperparts with blue-grey head and white-fringed black eye-mask. Vivid blue wattles sit under heavy black bill; these start off as lilac on juveniles. Wings short and rounded, complemented by long, broad, drooping tail. Long black legs and dark brown iris. Sexes indistinguishable. **DISTRIBUTION** Restricted to NI and adjacent offshore islands, with best viewing at Pureora Forest Park, Tiritiri Matangi and Kāpiti Islands. **HABITS AND HABITAT** Poor flier but still very mobile; long, powerful legs help it hop between branches. On mainland can be primarily found in diverse native hardwood forest with emergent podocarp trees. Fruits and leaves make up main component of diet. Song

Juvenile

melodious and mournful, reminiscent of an organ; can be heard kilometres away, most often at dawn and dusk. **CONSERVATION** Endemic/Nationally Increasing. From a low of 330 pairs in 1999, population increase to over 2,000 pairs in 2022 can be credited to diligent translocations and pest control. High risk of predation of eggs, chicks and females during nesting, by ship rats and possums. Darker plumaged and orange-wattled **South Island Kōkako** C. *cinereus* reclassified as Data Deficient in 2011 after being declared extinct in 2004. Despite no recent solid evidence, sightings continue to be reported.

Adult

North Island Saddleback ■ *Philesturnus rufusater* 25cm
(tīeke)

DESCRIPTION Medium-sized, glossy black songbird with diagnostic golden-edged chestnut saddle across wings. Rump and tail-coverts match saddle colour; fleshy red wattles sit at base of bill. Juveniles and females alike, with smaller wattles than in adult male. **DISTRIBUTION** Found in and around pest-proof sanctuaries across NI and some offshore islands such as Tiritiri Matangi. **HABITS AND HABITAT** Weak flier, keeping close to the ground and foraging noisily among leaf litter in search of invertebrates. Song can be reminiscent of car alarm. **CONSERVATION** Endemic/Recovering. Eradicated on mainland by mammalian predators in early 1900s. Recovery efforts and translocations from last population on Taranga Island have allowed species to flourish once again.

South Island Saddleback ■ *Philesturnus carunculatus* 25cm
(tīeke)

DESCRIPTION Lacks the golden edge to saddle of North Island Saddleback (above). Juveniles chocolate-brown all over (often called 'jackbirds'). **DISTRIBUTION** Located exclusively on pest-free islands around SI. Key sites are Ulva Island, Pukenui/Anchor Island in Fiordland, and Blumine and Motuara Islands in Marlborough Sounds. **HABITS AND HABITAT** Utilizes wedge-shaped bill to chip away at rotten wood. Prefers insects but takes nectar and fruits. Calls range from loud chattering to soft chirps, one written as *ti-e-ke-ke*, for which Māori named it. **CONSERVATION** Endemic/Recovering. Saved from extinction in 1964 after last refuge on Big South Cape Island was invaded by rats. 36 birds were moved to nearby islands. Attempts to re-establish on mainland in Brook Waimārama and Orokonui Ecosanctuaries have seen mixed results.

Juvenile

Adult

Hihi ▪ *Notiomystis cincta* 18cm ⓔ
(Stitchbird)

DESCRIPTION Unusual songbird with striking plumage. Male features black head and breast, white ear-tufts and vivid yellow shoulder-patches running down on to chest. Female dull brown in comparison, but both adults have fine, slightly decurved black bill; dark wings with white bar and buff outer edge; and black tail outlined in brown, often held erect. Iris black and slender legs pink to black. Juveniles similar to female but greyer and with yellow gape. **DISTRIBUTION** Natural population once existed across NI, but after heavy decline in 1800s they only remained on Hauturu/Little Barrier Island. Due to tireless translocations, birds now established on Tiritiri Matangi and Kapiti Islands, as well as Maungatautari, Rotokare, Bushy Park and Zealandia mainland sanctuaries. **HABITS AND HABITAT** Indicator species for health of native forests, requiring mature trees for

Female

sufficient food sources and nesting sites. Complex breeding system can involve multiple male and female partners (polygynandrous). Unique in being the only bird species to mate face to face. Primarily nectar feeders but also takes fruits and invertebrates. Main male call a piercing trisyllabic whistle; both sexes make *titch* contact call. **CONSERVATION** Endemic/Nationally Vulnerable. Re-established populations require supplementary sugar-water feeding and artificial nesting boxes to flourish in absence of pristine habitat – not all attempts have succeeded.

Male

Australian Magpie ■ *Gymnorhina tibicen* 37–43cm
(makipai)

DESCRIPTION Predominantly black, with white patches on hindneck, wings, vent and rump. Back colour varies between white-backed and black-backed forms, which also interbreed. Eye crimson, and wedge-shaped bill silver tipped in black. Female has mottled grey back. Juveniles grey in lieu of black, with darker bills and eyes.

DISTRIBUTION Introduced from Australia in 1860–'70s; now widespread across mainland.

HABITS AND HABITAT Resident across open hill country with sufficient trees to nest and roost in, as well as urban parks and gardens. Readily dive bombs potential threats (including humans) that approach near active nests. Distinctive call best written as *quardle-oodle-ardle-wardle-doodle.*

CONSERVATION Introduced and naturalized. Opportunistic; known to prey on native fauna.

Female white-backed morph

Rook ■ *Corvus frugilegus* 45–47cm

DESCRIPTION Only member of crow family in modern NZ. Large, glossy black bird with bluish sheen. Face bare, revealing whitish skin between dark eye and heavy slate-grey bill. Wings broad, with primaries resembling fingers. Juveniles have feathered face and black bill. **DISTRIBUTION** Introduced from Europe in 1860s; scattered across inland NI and SI in low numbers.

HABITS AND HABITAT Found in areas of open country and woodland. Colonial nester, known to form large 'rookeries' in stands of tall trees. Majority of diet invertebrates. Call a typical hoarse *kaaw-kaaw.*

CONSERVATION Introduced and naturalized. Persecuted as unwanted organism in NZ for its apparent damage to crop yields.

Mohua ■ *Mohoua orchocephala* 15cm (e)
(Yellowhead)

Female

Male

DESCRIPTION Small forest bird sometimes dubbed 'the canary of the bush', due to its tuneful call and deep yellow head and breast. Upperparts and spiked tail feathers olive-brown with clean divide along nape from yellow. Lower belly and vent off-white, pointed bill and long legs black, and iris dark. Female appears less bright than male, and juveniles have dark crown and flanks. **DISTRIBUTION** SI endemic, but lost in 95 per cent of former range. Hotspots include Haast's Pass and Glenorchy in C Otago, the Catlins and Fiordland. Translocated successfully to Whenua Hou/Codfish Island and Ulva Island near Rakiura/Stewart Island, Pigeon Island/Wawahi-Waka in Lake Wakatipu, and Blumine Island in Marlborough Sounds. **HABITS AND HABITAT** Tends to move as noisy flocks high through the canopy of mature native forest. Often associates with the Brown Creeper (opposite) and kākāriki species. Preferred nest sites are tree cavities, where 1–4 eggs are laid and incubated by female. One of host species for the Long-tailed Cuckoo (p. 30). Insectivorous; feeding methods include gleaning, scratching among leaf litter, and foraging on tree branches using spiked tail as prop. Song a cheerful staccato trill accompanied by chirping calls. **CONSERVATION** Endemic/Declining. Pest control has allowed mainland populations to stabilize, with numbers in Westland's Landsborough valley increasing 30-fold to nearly 500 individuals over 21 years of monitoring, with similar results across its range.

Whitehead ■ *Mohoua albicilla* 15cm (e)
(pōpokatea)

DESCRIPTION Compact, chocolate-brown songbird with head appearing as if it were dipped in white paint. Breast pale; buff flanks and belly. Female and juveniles have greyer head than male. Slender legs and short bill black. **DISTRIBUTION** Occurs only in NI, as well as adjacent islands including Hauturu/Little Barrier and Kapiti Islands. Locally common S of Waikato. **HABITS AND HABITAT** Found in mature native forest and shrubland, and increasingly in exotic pine plantations. Flocks comprising small family groups systematically glean insects from trees. Male's song a powerful descending series of chirps. Often heard first with near-constant chattering.
CONSERVATION Endemic/Not Threatened. Drastic early decline from predation and habitat clearance is being halted by ongoing translocations and pest control.

Juvenile

Adult

Brown Creeper ■ *Mohoua novaeseelandiae* 13cm (e)
(pīpīpī)

DESCRIPTION Tiny songster. Face and nape grey; upperparts brownish with rufous on crown, wings and tail. Underparts creamy-brown, turning paler around throat. Faint white stripe trails behind eye. Short bill and slender legs pinkish-grey.
DISTRIBUTION Only found in SI, Rakiura/Stewart Island, and adjacent offshore islands such as Ulva Island. Fairly widespread, with highest numbers near Southern Alps and in Marlborough Sounds. **HABITS AND HABITAT** Gregarious bird of native forest, forming extended family flocks while foraging in the canopy. Mobs parasitic Long-tailed Cuckoos (p. 30) in summer; also its target host. Diet primarily invertebrates. Song comprises undulating liquid notes, and call a typical chirp. **CONSERVATION** Endemic/Not Threatened.

New Zealand Fantail ■ *Rhipidura fuliginosa* 16cm e
(pīwakawaka)

DESCRIPTION ssp. *placabilis* (North Island), *fuliginosa* (South Island), *penita* (Chatham Island). Iconic, charming little bird with two distinct forms. Most common 'pied' morph appears chocolate-brown above and buff below. Head dark grey with white markings above button eyes resembling eyebrows; broad white band across chin. Long black and white tail distinctive. Immature plumage less defined, with orangey colouring below and on wings and brows. 'Black' morph less common; differs in being completely blackish-brown including tail, but sometimes has white spot behind eye. Short bill and legs black.
DISTRIBUTION Common throughout NI, SI and Rakiura/Stewart Island, as well as nearby offshore islands and Rēkohu/Chatham Islands. Black morph makes up about 5 per cent of SI birds; very rare in NI, and absent from Chathams. **HABITS AND HABITAT** Occurs in range of environments: both native and exotic forests, well-vegetated parks and gardens, orchards and shrubland, to name a few. Often follows people for their tendency to stir up flying insects, which are captured with aerobatic skill. Vulnerable to cold weather and roosts communally, birds huddle together to conserve heat. Call a series of squeaky *cheeps*, song culminates in high-pitched chattering similar to turning knob of a rusty faucet. **CONSERVATION** Endemic/Not Threatened. Has coped remarkably well with modification of NZ's environments, but still occasionally predated upon by mammalian pests.

Black morph   Pied morph

Tomtit ■ *Petroica macrocephala* 13cm Ⓔ
(miromiro – N, ngirungiru – S)

DESCRIPTION ssp. *toitoi* (North Island), *macrocephala* (South Island), *chathamensis* (Chatham Island), *dannefaerdi* (Snares Island), *marrineri* (Auckland Island). Small songbird with large head and tiny, pointed bill with white patch above base. Adult male has black upperparts including head and throat, with clean line separating from white underparts. Outside of NI, males have yellow colouration on breast, varying in brightness between subspecies. White wing-bar prominent; legs black and feet orange. Females similar except with grey-brown colouring above as opposed to black. Juveniles duller with faint streaking on head and smudgy breasts. Both sexes of Snares Islands subspecies have entirely black plumage. **DISTRIBUTION** Widespread resident on NI, SI and Rakiura/Stewart Islands, including some nearby offshore islands. Found on Pitt, Rangatira and Māngere Islands in Rēkohu/Chathams group, as well as on Snares and Auckland Islands. **HABITS AND HABITAT** Locally common in mature native forest; increasingly in exotic pine plantations. Birds rarely venture outside preferred habitat, but known to disperse long distances. Unafraid of humans, often approaching them to investigate. Mostly insectivorous, tending to wait on perch and scan for prey before pouncing. Male song a brief, rapid *swee-oly-oly-oly-ee*. High-pitched one-note contact calls also often heard. **CONSERVATION** Endemic/Not Threatened. High mortality rate of egg clutches and brooding females in areas lacking pest control.

Adult Snares Island subspecies

Adult male South Island subspecies

North Island subspecies male (left) and female on nest

North Island Robin ■ *Petroica longipes* 18cm
(toutouwai)

DESCRIPTION Small, upright songbird with long black legs. Male streaked slate-grey with white belly. Female lighter grey with smaller white belly-patch. Both sexes have pale eye-ring and white frontal band above narrow black bill. Hops characteristically. **DISTRIBUTION** Parts of C NI, as well as Hauturu/Little Barrier and Kapiti Islands. Reintroduced to many pest-free sites, including Tiritiri Matangi and Zealandia. **HABITS AND HABITAT** Occurs in established native and exotic forest, and areas of tall scrub. Most foraging takes place in leaf litter. Very territorial; males defend their patch by giving powerful and varied song from chosen perch year round. **CONSERVATION** Endemic/Declining. Land clearance by early settlers to NZ has caused huge reduction in range.

South Island Robin ■ *Petroica australis* 18cm
(kakaruai)

DESCRIPTION ssp. *australis* (South Island), *rakiura* (Stewart Island). Dark grey male has cream-coloured belly-patch (reduced in lighter female). Large, curious eyes black, as well as long, slender legs. Juveniles have faint streaking and indistinct pale underside. **DISTRIBUTION** Widespread across SI, Rakiura/Stewart Island and surrounding islands; absent from most of Canterbury, Otago and the Catlins. **HABITS AND HABITAT** Found in mature native forest, scrubland and exotic plantations. Very confiding to regular human visitors. Diet of invertebrates and small fruits, the latter particularly in drier periods. Both sexes make loud *songs and* calls. **CONSERVATION** Endemic/Declining. Eggs, chicks and sitting females at high risk of predation, which can lead to male-biased population. Reintroduced to several sites.

Black Robin ■ *Petroica traversi* 15cm

(karure, kakaruia)

DESCRIPTION Small, rotund bird. Both sexes have entirely sooty-black plumage, dark brown iris and slender pinkish legs. Small black bill has tiny whiskers at base (rictal bristles). Juveniles can be told by brown flight feathers and subtle streaking on crown. **DISTRIBUTION** Restricted to Rēkohu/Chatham Islands, where it was extirpated apart from on Little Māngere Island (rediscovered there in 1938). All birds translocated after extensive research to more secure Māngere Island in 1976. Once numbers increased sufficiently, new population was established on Rangatira/South East Island. Both populations located on restricted access reserves under management of DOC. **HABITS AND HABITAT** Curious denizen of native island forest interiors, predominately foraging in leaf litter for various small invertebrates. Nests annually in spring and summer, with cup-like twig nest typically constructed within 2m of the ground. Female lays and incubates two eggs. Call a simple series of whistling notes, mainly given by male. **CONSERVATION** Endemic/Nationally Critical. Survivor of one of the most impressive conservation comebacks in history, when the late Don Merton ran a team to translocate the last remaining individuals to Māngere Island while also fostering the chicks in Tomtit (p. 149) nests on Rangatira Island. In 1980 the population was down to a mere five individuals, including one breeding pair. All birds alive today stem from one female, dubbed 'Old Blue'. Inbreeding led to further (yet manageable) issues, including a strange trend of laying eggs on the edge of their nests. Numbers today are stable on Rangatira and the total population sits around 300 birds.

New Zealand Pipit ▪ *Anthus novaeseelandiae* 18cm
(pīhoihoi)

DESCRIPTION ssp. *novaseelandiae*, *chathamensis* (Chatham Island), *aucklandicus* (Auckland and Campbell Islands), *steindachneri* (Antipodes Island). Plain, long-legged songbird with bold white brow. Cream underparts accented by dark streaking on breast, and grey-brown mottling above. Fine blackish bill meets dark eye-stripe. Flicks tail while walking unlike Skylark (below). **DISTRIBUTION** Widespread across mainland NZ; other subspecies resident on Rēkohu/ Chatham Islands and subantarctic islands. **HABITS AND HABITAT** Favours rugged coastline, open country and alpine zones. Forages at ground level for seeds, grains and invertebrates. Generally unafraid of people. Gives harsh *tzweep* year round. **CONSERVATION** Endemic/Declining. Threatened on mainland, where pastures are overdeveloped and pesticides increasingly used.

Eurasian Skylark ▪ *Alauda arvensis* 18cm
(kairaka)

DESCRIPTION Ground-dwelling songbird. Creamy underparts and grey-brown above, with buff highlights and dark striations across head, back and breast. Broad wings have white trailing edge as well as on outer-tail feathers. Legs pink, and sturdy bill dull yellow. Small head-crest can be lowered. **DISTRIBUTION** Common throughout mainland NZ and Chatham Islands after 1860s introduction. **HABITS AND HABITAT** Occurs in areas of open country, farmland, tussock grassland and sub-alpine zones. Diet of seeds, cereals, clovers and weeds. Iconic melodious song given by males high in sky, often impossible to spot. Generally wary of people. Other call a liquid *chirrup*, also usually made in flight. **CONSERVATION** Introduced and naturalized.

Fernbird ■ *Poodytes punctatus* 18cm (e)

(koroātito: N, mātātā: S, mātā)

DESCRIPTION ssp. *vealeae* (North Island), *punctatus* (South Island), *stewartianus* (Stewart Island), *wilsoni* (Codfish Island), *caudatus* (Snares). Small, scruffy passerine with short, rounded wings and characteristic long, fern-like tail. Plumage brown above fading to white on throat and underside. Streaked black overall with rufous crown and white supercilium. Intensity, size and colouration vary between forms. Snares birds are largest and plainer brown overall. **DISTRIBUTION** Widespread but patchy across mainland NZ, Rakiura/Stewart Island, The Snares, and some offshore islands (translocated to Tiritiri Matangi). Absent from most of Canterbury, Wellington and Wairarapa. **HABITS AND**

HABITAT Bird of scrubland and wetlands, both inland and coastal; spends a majority of its time under dense vegetation cover, skulking not unlike a mouse. Snares birds can be seen foraging in penguin and sea-lion colonies. Diet mainly insects and other small invertebrates. Main call is a short but piercing *u-tick*. **CONSERVATION** Endemic/Declining. Habitat loss and predation are main factors. The **Chatham Island Fernbird** *P. rufescens* became extinct at the end of the 1800s.

Snares subspecies

North Island subspecies

South Island subspecies

Welcome Swallow ▪ *Hirundo neoxena* 14–16cm
(warou)

DESCRIPTION ssp. *neoxena*. Small, fast-flying bird; metallic blue-black above, pale orange forehead and throat with black eye-patch, and cream underparts. Wings long and pointed; deeply forked tail has white horizontal band. Black bill and short, slender legs. Sexes alike; juveniles distinguished by yellow gape and muted plumage. Smaller **Tree Martin** *Petrochelidon nigricans* and **Fairy Martin** *P. ariel* are vagrants. **DISTRIBUTION** Arrived naturally from Australia in 1950s and soon became well established throughout NZ. **HABITS AND HABITAT** Hawks for flying insects over waterbodies: lakes, rivers and estuaries, as well as open fields. Nest formed from mud and saliva on sides of cliffs and buildings. Gives *zip* call and varied chittery song. **CONSERVATION** Native/Not Threatened.

Juveniles and adults interspersed

Adult

Silvereye ▪ *Zosterops lateralis* 12cm
(tauhou)

DESCRIPTION ssp. *lateralis*. Distinctive for olive-green head and bold white eye-ring. Throat and breast pale grey, darkening over mantle. Flanks peach and underside cream to white. Green plumage resumes on wings and rump; flight and tail feathers dark. Grey bill finely pointed, and legs grey-brown. **DISTRIBUTION** Very common in NZ. Self-colonized from Australia in 1850s and soon became widespread. **HABITS AND**

HABITAT Moves through well-vegetated areas such as orchards, parks and forests in tight-knit flocks (larger in winter). Feeds on leaves, fruits, insects and nectar. Main call a sweet *tsew* or a cry reminiscent of a tiny horse's whinny; song consists of various high-pitched twitters and warbles. **CONSERVATION** Native/Not Threatened.

Common Myna ■ *Acridotheres tristis* 23–26cm
(maina)

DESCRIPTION Head black with bare yellow patch of skin behind yellow eye. Brown overall with white wing-bar, underwings and tail-tip evident in flight. Bill and legs bright yellow, sexes alike. **DISTRIBUTION** Restricted to NI; abundant in N but found as far S as Wellington. Introduced in 1870s to NZ; native to S Asia. **HABITS AND HABITAT** Lives in many different environments especially urban. Aggressive towards other species within territory; destroys eggs and nestlings if discovered. Omnivorous. Call varies; often a melodic but harsh squawking. **CONSERVATION** Introduced and naturalized. Regarded as invasive, and known to compete with and prey upon native species.

Common Starling ■ *Sturnus vulgaris* 20–22cm
(tāringi)

DESCRIPTION ssp. *vulgaris*. Glossy black songbird with purple and green sheen, and body feathers tipped with white spots that wear off in winter. Bill yellow (black in winter) and legs pink. Sexes similar; juveniles grey-brown with pale throat. **DISTRIBUTION** Abundant across NZ after 1862 introduction to control insects. Natural range spans from Europe to C Asia. **HABITS AND HABITAT** Lives primarily in urban and open country in close association with humans. Forms vast, twisting flocks at dusk while travelling to night roost. Commonly seen searching for seeds and insects in grass. Call a descending whistle and song, a mix of clicks, wheezes and gurgles; each individual has its own variation and they are impressive mimics of other birds. **CONSERVATION** Introduced and naturalized.

Immature

Non-breeding adult

Breeding male

Female   Male with chick

Eurasian Blackbird
■ *Turdus merula* 24–27cm
(manu pango)

DESCRIPTION ssp. *merula*. Familiar long-tailed thrush. Male glossy black, bright orange bill and eye-ring stand out against body. Female has dark brown plumage with grey throat, and juveniles brown with lighter speckling; compare to Song Thrush (below). **DISTRIBUTION** Potentially the most widely distributed bird in NZ. Introduced from Europe to both main islands during 1860s–'70s, where it is now abundant. **HABITS AND HABITAT** Comfortable in gardens, farmland, exotic plantations and native forest. Established pairs territorial. Diet of invertebrates; sometimes pauses to 'listen' for food beneath the ground. Male's song a low, flute-like warble, always from high perch. *Chinks* and *chooks* make up array of calls. **CONSERVATION** Introduced and naturalized.

Male

Song Thrush ■ *Turdus philomelos* 21–23cm
(manu-kai-hua-rakau)

DESCRIPTION Small, upright thrush. Underside cream peppered with dark brown chevrons. Uniform upperparts and intricate facial markings warmer brown. Bill grey with yellow gape, iris black and legs pale pink. Juveniles similar, with golden haze over breast and face. **DISTRIBUTION** Fairly common across NZ. Introduced from Europe in 1860s–'70s, and quickly established on most outlying islands. **HABITS AND HABITAT** Found readily in gardens, orchards, parks and farmland areas. Omnivorous, but snails are preferred prey, broken by smashing them against hard surfaces with flick of the head. Known for melodic, repetitive song, which can be heard year round. **CONSERVATION** Introduced and naturalized.

Adult

House Sparrow ■ *Passer domesticus* 15–16cm
(tiu)

DESCRIPTION ssp. *domesticus*. Familiar small passerine. Male black-streaked chestnut-brown above; underparts, rump and crown grey. Cheeks pale with black eye-stripe and bib. Robust beak yellowish to black (breeding male). Legs dull pink. Female and juveniles show lighter brown tones, with beige brow. **DISTRIBUTION** Became abundant nationwide soon after introduction in 1860s. Native to Eurasia, but has also expanded across America, Australia and S Africa. **HABITS AND HABITAT** Takes quickly to any environment except dense bush and high mountains. Diet mainly seeds and grains; discarded food scraps favoured in urban areas. Remarkably sedentary, with large flocks assembling in late summer. Both song and calls comprise various standard cheeps and chirps. **CONSERVATION** Introduced and naturalized.

Female

Male

Dunnock ■ *Prunella modularis* 13.5–14cm
(Hedge Accentor)

DESCRIPTION Male and female brown with grey crown, neck and underparts. Dark streaks accent face and run across wings and back. Black bill slender and pointed, legs orange-brown and iris crimson. Juveniles resemble adult plumage except paler and with heavier streaking. **DISTRIBUTION** Widespread across NZ although scarcer N of Waikato. Introduced from England in 1860s–'90s; native range Eurasia. **HABITS AND HABITAT** Solitary bird often overlooked, foraging alongside vegetation in parks, gardens and open country. Complex mating system involving polyandrous females and male competition; territory size depends on food availability. Mainly insectivorous, taking chiefly spiders, ants, flies and beetles. Song a pleasant warble; contact call a sharp *tseep*. **CONSERVATION** Introduced and naturalized.

Adult

Eurasian Chaffinch ■ *Fringilla coelebs* 14–15cm
(pahirini)

DESCRIPTION Brightly coloured songbird. Male distinctive with pinkish-orange breast and face, as well as blue-grey nape and black-fronted crown. Female has more brown and beige tones. Both sexes have stout grey bill, olive-green rump, and black wings with bold white wing-bars and tail feaathers. **DISTRIBUTION** Common across NZ after introduction from Europe in 1860s. Also originates from N Africa and W Asia. **HABITS AND HABITAT** Mainly occupies parks, gardens, open country and exotic forest. Diet of seeds,

grains and, during breeding season, invertebrates. Males and females sometimes create segregated flocks in winter. *Chink* call as well as male's *chip-chip-chip chooee-chooee-cheeoo* song often heard before bird is seen. **CONSERVATION** Introduced and naturalized.

Male

Female

European Greenfinch
■ *Chloris chloris* 15–16cm

DESCRIPTION Largest of introduced finches. Male exhibits yellow-green plumage of varying intensity, with grey accents. Female and young birds drabber, with brown tones on back. Large conical bill and legs are pink. Pale yellow edging on wings and forked tail evident in flight. **DISTRIBUTION** Introduced in 1860s and now common and widespread across NZ. Natural range Europe, N Africa and SW Asia. **HABITS AND HABITAT** Sociable species, rarely solitary, favouring gardens, farmland, orchards and pine plantations. Capable of cracking larger seeds than other finches. Male's song a fast-paced, repetitive *dit-dit-dit-dit tew tew tew* interspersed by loud *dzweee* call. **CONSERVATION** Introduced and naturalized.

Male

Female

European Goldfinch

■ *Carduelis carduelis* 12–13cm
(kōurarini)

Juvenile

DESCRIPTION ssp. *britannica*. Tiny songbird. Adults unmistakable, with bold red and white face, and black extending back from crown to nape. Upperparts, flanks and breast buff-brown; paler underneath. Flight feathers black with white tips and golden panels. Bill pale pink, ending in fine point. Sexes similar. **DISTRIBUTION** Common across NZ after introduction from Europe from 1860s. Naturally occurring throughout Europe, N Africa and W Asia. **HABITS AND HABITAT** Found in gardens, parks, fields and almost anywhere apart from dense native forest. Preferred food is seeds, especially those of weeds and thistles. Melodic cheeps, tinkles and twitters make up its repertoire. **CONSERVATION** Introduced and naturalized.

Adult

Redpoll ■ *Acanthis flammea* 11.5–12.5cm

DESCRIPTION Tiny, tan-brown with dark streaking above and red crown (absent on juveniles). Adult male has rosy hues around throat and breast, strongest while breeding. Black lores and chin with short yellow bill. Pale wing-bars and undertail-coverts seen in flight. **DISTRIBUTION** Common nationwide, generally in higher numbers further S. European introduction, released in 1860s. **HABITS AND HABITAT** Favours open country such as farmland and shrubland. Enters parks and gardens periodically in search of seeds from trees and grasses. Commonly utters staccato *chich-ich-ich* during buoyant flight, as well as a *tswee* between individuals.

Male

Female

Female

Yellowhammer

■ *Emberiza citrinella* 16–16.5cm
(hurukōwhai)

DESCRIPTION Exotic perching bird; head bright yellow with brown facial markings. Dark-streaked chestnut above with rufous rump, and dull yellow underside. Long, forked tail edged white, visible in flight. Stubby grey-black bill and pinkish legs. Plumage subdued in female and juveniles; latter also more heavily streaked. **DISTRIBUTION** Breeds across mainland NZ and surrounding islands after introduction in 1860s; naturally in Europe and NW Asia. **HABITS AND HABITAT** Favours rural open country and scrubland, but can be found in parks and gardens on occasion. Congregates in mixed flocks at feeding grounds in winter. Eats mainly seeds; invertebrates an important food source while breeding. Gives a *twick* contact call, and characteristic song of male akin to *chitty-chitty-chitty-swee*. **CONSERVATION** Introduced and naturalized.

Male

Cirl Bunting ■ *Emberiza cirlus* 15–16.5cm

DESCRIPTION Male stands out by bumblebee facial markings; dark eye-stripe with yellow on either side, dark crown and black throat. Dark-streaked chestnut above, with olive-green rump and chest-band on adult male. Stubby grey bill and pinkish legs. Female and juveniles browner and streakier. **DISTRIBUTION** Rare 1870s European introduction that never became widespread. Most sightings in SI regions of Nelson, Marlborough and Canterbury, but can appear anywhere sporadically across NZ. **HABITS AND HABITAT** Cryptic; can occur in dry scrubland, open country and woodlands. Diet of seeds and invertebrates foraged from the ground. Territorial and thought to be rather sedentary. Male gives a repetitive rattling song; also utters a sharp contact *tseep*. **CONSERVATION** Introduced and naturalized.

Female

Male

▪ Checklist of the Birds of New Zealand ▪

Sequence and taxonomy predominantly follow the Checklist of the Birds of New Zealand (5th edition), 2022, Ornithological Society of New Zealand Occasional Publication No. 1. There are minor tweaks in order to create a guide that is purpose-built for identification – useful for overseas visitors and locals, novice and experienced birders alike, and anyone ready to learn more.

Definitions of New Zealand status of the following 396 species:

E Endemic species. Breeds only in New Zealand, including species that have been declared extinct since 1800.

N Native species. Naturally occurring resident in New Zealand also breeding elsewhere.

C Colonizer. Recently (since 1950) self-established breeding species in New Zealand.

M Migrant. Seasonal non-breeding visitor to New Zealand, either on passage or for a portion of the year.

V Vagrant. Sporadic visitor to New Zealand with less than five individuals per year, often outside its expected range.

I Introduced and naturalized. Brought to New Zealand by humans and has become established, either intentionally or accidentally. Species that have been extirpated (such as Grey Partridge, Crimson Rosella, Red-vented Bulbul) or that are not established as feral (such as Muscovy Duck, Red Junglefowl) are not included.

Abbreviations of IUCN Red List worldwide status:

LC Least Concern
NT Near Threatened
VU Vulnerable
EN Endangered
CR Critically Endangered
EX Extinct

The relevant New Zealand Conservation status is also listed under the subheading 'Conservation' in the bird profiles throughout this book.

Common Name	Māori name	Scientific Name	Status	IUCN
Apterygidae (Kiwi)				
North Island Brown Kiwi	Kiwi-nui	Apteryx mantelli	E	VU
Okarito Brown Kiwi	Rowi	Apteryx rowi	E	VU
Southern Brown Kiwi	Tokoeka	Apteryx australis	E	VU
Little Spotted Kiwi	Kiwi Pukupuku	Apteryx owenii	E	NT
Great Spotted Kiwi	Roroa	Apteryx maxima	E	VU
Casuariidae (Emu)				
Emu		Dromaius novaehollandiae	I	LC
Anatidae (Ducks, Geese & Swans)				
Plumed Whistling-duck		Dendrocygna eytoni	V	LC
Mute Swan	Wāna	Cygnus olor	I	LC
Black Swan	Kakīānau	Cygnus atratus	N	LC

Common Name	Māori name	Scientific Name	Status	IUCN
Cape Barren Goose		*Cereopsis novaehollandiae*	I	LC
Greylag Goose	Kuihi	*Anser anser*	I	LC
Canada Goose	Kuihi	*Branta canadensis*	I	LC
Pink-eared Duck		*Malacorhynchus membranaceus*	V	LC
Paradise Shelduck	Pūtangitangi	*Tadorna variegata*	E	LC
Australian Shelduck		*Tadorna tadornoides*	V	LC
Auckland Island Merganser	Miuweka	*Mergus australis*	E	EX
Australian Wood Duck		*Chenonetta jubata*	C	LC
Blue Duck	Whio	*Hymenolaimus malacorhynchos*	E	EN
Grey Teal	Tētē-moroiti	*Anas gracilis*	N	LC
Chestnut Teal		*Anas castanea*	V	LC
Brown Teal	Pāteke	*Anas chlorotis*	E	NT
Auckland Island Teal	Tētē Kākāriki	*Anas aucklandica*	E	NT
Campbell Island Teal		*Anas nesiotis*	E	VU
Northern Pintail		*Anas acuta*	V	LC
Mallard	Rakiraki	*Anas platyrhynchos*	I	LC
Grey Duck	Pārera	*Anas superciliosa*	N	LC
Australasian Shoveler	Kuruwhengi	*Spatula rhynchotis*	N	LC
Northern Shoveler		*Spatula clypeata*	V	LC
Australian White-eyed Duck	Karakahia	*Aythya australis*	V	LC
New Zealand Scaup	Pāpango	*Aythya novaeseelandiae*	E	LC
Numididae (Guineafowl)				
Helmeted Guineafowl		*Numida meleagris*	I	LC
Odontophoridae (New World Quails)				
California Quail	Tīkaokao	*Callipepla californica*	I	LC
Phasianidae (Pheasants & Allies)				
New Zealand Quail	Koreke	*Coturnix novaezelandiae*	E	EX
Brown Quail	Kuera	*Synoicus ypsilophorus*	I	LC
Chukar		*Alectoris chukar*	I	LC
Indian Peafowl	Pīkao	*Pavo cristatus*	I	LC
Wild Turkey	Korukoru	*Meleagris gallopavo*	I	LC
Common Pheasant	Peihana	*Phasianus colchicus*	I	LC
Podicipedidae (Grebes)				
Australasian Crested Grebe	Pūteketeke	*Podiceps cristatus*	N	LC
New Zealand Dabchick	Weweia	*Poliocephalus rufopectus*	E	LC
Hoary-headed Grebe	Taihoropī	*Poliocephalus poliocephalus*	C	LC
Australasian Little Grebe	Tokitokipio	*Tachybaptus novaehollandiae*	C	LC
Columbidae (Pigeons & Doves)				
Rock Pigeon	Kererū Aropari	*Columba livia*	I	LC
Barbary Dove		*Streptopelia risoria*	I	LC
Spotted Dove		*Streptopelia chinensis*	I	LC
Rose-crowned Fruit-dove		*Ptilinopus regina*	V	LC
New Zealand Pigeon	Kererū	*Hemiphaga novaeseelandiae*	E	LC
Chatham Island Pigeon	Parea	*Hemiphaga chathamensis*	E	VU
Cuculidae (Cuckoos)				
Oriental Cuckoo		*Cuculus optatus*	V	LC
Pallid Cuckoo		*Cacomantis pallidus*	V	LC
Fan-tailed Cuckoo		*Cacomantis flabelliformis*	V	LC
Shining Cuckoo	Pīpīwharauroa	*Chrysococcyx lucidus*	N	LC
Long-tailed Cuckoo	Koekoeā	*Urodynamis taitensis*	E	LC
Channel-billed Cuckoo		*Scythrops novaehollandiae*	V	LC

Common Name	Māori name	Scientific Name	Status	IUCN
Apodidae (Swifts)				
White-throated Needletail		Hirundapus caudacutus	V	LC
Fork-tailed Swift		Apus pacificus	V	LC
Rallidae (Rails, Crakes & Coots)				
Corncrake		Crex crex	V	LC
Auckland Island Rail		Lewinia muelleri	E	VU
Banded Rail	Moho Pererū	Gallirallus philippensis	N	LC
Dieffenbach's Rail	Moeriki	Gallirallus dieffenbachii	E	EX
Weka	Weka	Gallirallus australis	E	VU
Chatham Island Rail	Mātirakahu	Cabalus modestus	E	EX
Australian Crake		Porzana fluminea	V	LC
Spotless Crake	Pūweto	Zapornia tabuensis	N	LC
Marsh Crake	Kotoreke	Zapornia pusilla	N	LC
Common Moorhen		Gallinula chloropus	V	LC
Dusky Moorhen		Gallinula tenebrosa	V	LC
Black-tailed Native-hen		Tribonyx ventralis	V	LC
Pukeko	Pūkeko	Porphyrio melanotus	N	LC
South Island Takahē	Takahē	Porphyrio hochstetteri	E	EN
Australian Coot		Fulica atra	N	LC
Gruidae (Cranes)				
Crane sp. (Brolga/Sarus Crane)		Grus sp. indet. (rubicunda/antigone)	V	LC/ VU
Haematopodidae (Oystercatchers)				
Variable Oystercatcher	Tōrea Pango	Haematopus unicolor	E	LC
South Island Pied Oystercatcher	Tōrea	Haematopus finschi	E	LC
Chatham Island Oystercatcher	Tōrea Tai	Haematopus chathamensis	E	EN
Recurvirostridae (Stilts & Avocets)				
Pied Stilt	Poaka	Himantopus himantopus	N	LC
Black Stilt	Kakī	Himantopus novaezelandiae	E	CR
Red-necked Avocet	Piwari	Recurvirostra novaehollandiae	V	LC
Charadriidae (Plovers)				
Pacific Golden Plover	Kuriri	Pluvialis fulva	M	LC
American Golden Plover		Pluvialis dominicus	V	LC
Grey Plover		Pluvialis squatarola	V	LC
New Zealand Dotterel	Tūturiwhatu	Charadrius obscurus	E	NT
Semipalmated Plover		Charadrius semipalmatus	V	LC
Red-capped Plover		Charadrius ruficapillus	V	LC
Banded Dotterel	Pohowera	Charadrius bicinctus	E	NT
Siberian Sand Plover		Charadrius mongolus	V	LC
Tibetan Sand Plover		Charadrius atrifrons	V	LC
Greater Sand Plover		Charadrius leschenaultii	V	LC
Oriental Dotterel		Charadrius veredus	V	LC
Wrybill	Ngutu Pare	Anarhynchus frontalis	E	VU
Black-fronted Dotterel		Elseyornis melanops	N	LC
Shore Plover	Tuturuatu	Thinornis novaeseelandiae	E	EN
Red-kneed Dotterel		Erythrogonys cinctus	V	LC
Masked Lapwing		Vanellus miles	N	LC
Rostratulidae (Painted Snipes)				
Australian Painted Snipe		Rostratula australis	V	EN

Common Name	Māori name	Scientific Name	Status	IUCN
Scolopacidae (Sandpipers & Snipes)				
Upland Sandpiper		*Bartramia longicauda*	V	LC
Eastern Curlew		*Numenius madagascariensis*	V	EN
Eurasian Whimbrel		*Numenius phaeopus*	M	LC
American Whimbrel		*Numenius hudsonicus*	V	LC
Little Whimbrel		*Numenius minutus*	V	LC
Bristle-thighed Curlew		*Numenius tahitiensis*	V	NT
Bar-tailed Godwit	Kuaka	*Limosa lapponica*	N	NT
Black-tailed Godwit		*Limosa limosa*	V	NT
Hudsonian Godwit		*Limosa haemastica*	V	LC
Ruddy Turnstone		*Arenaria interpres*	M	LC
Great Knot		*Calidris tenuirostris*	V	EN
Red Knot	Huahou	*Calidris canutus*	N	NT
Ruff		*Calidris pugnax*	V	LC
Broad-billed Sandpiper		*Calidris falcinellus*	V	LC
Sharp-tailed Sandpiper	Kohutapu	*Calidris acuminata*	M	VU
Stilt Sandpiper		*Calidris himantopus*	V	LC
Curlew Sandpiper		*Calidris ferruginea*	V	NT
Long-toed Stint		*Calidris subminuta*	V	LC
Red-necked Stint		*Calidris ruficollis*	M	NT
Sanderling		*Calidris alba*	V	LC
Dunlin		*Calidris alpina*	V	LC
Baird's Sandpiper		*Calidris bairdii*	V	LC
Little Stint		*Calidris minuta*	V	LC
Least Sandpiper		*Calidris minutilla*	V	LC
White-rumped Sandpiper		*Calidris fuscicollis*	V	LC
Buff-breasted Sandpiper		*Calidris subruficollis*	V	NT
Pectoral Sandpiper		*Calidris melanotos*	V	LC
Semipalmated Sandpiper		*Calidris pusilla*	V	NT
Western Sandpiper		*Calidris mauri*	V	LC
Asiatic Dowitcher		*Limnodromus semipalmatus*	V	NT
North Island Snipe		*Coenocorypha barrierensis*	E	EX
South Island Snipe	Tutukiwi	*Coenocorypha iredalei*	E	EX
Chatham Island Snipe		*Coenocorypha pusilla*	E	VU
Snares Island Snipe	Tutukiwi	*Coenocorypha huegeli*	E	NT
Subantarctic Snipe		*Coenocorypha aucklandica*	E	NT
Japanese Snipe		*Gallinago hardwickii*	V	NT
Grey Phalarope		*Phalaropus fulicarius*	V	LC
Red-necked Phalarope		*Phalaropus lobatus*	V	LC
Wilson's Phalarope		*Phalaropus tricolor*	V	LC
Terek Sandpiper		*Xenus cinereus*	V	LC
Common Sandpiper		*Actitis hypoleucos*	V	LC
Grey-tailed Tattler		*Tringa brevipes*	V	NT
Wandering Tattler		*Tringa incana*	V	LC
Lesser Yellowlegs		*Tringa flavipes*	V	LC
Common Greenshank		*Tringa nebularia*	V	LC
Marsh Sandpiper		*Tringa stagnatilis*	V	LC
Glareolidae (Pratincoles)				
Oriental Pratincole		*Glareola maldivarum*	V	LC
Stercorariidae (Skuas)				
Brown Skua	Hākoakoa	*Stercorarius antarcticus*	N	LC

Common Name	Māori name	Scientific Name	Status	IUCN
South Polar Skua		*Stercorarius maccormicki*	M	LC
Pomarine Skua		*Stercorarius pomarinus*	M	LC
Arctic Skua		*Stercorarius parasiticus*	M	LC
Long-tailed Skua		*Stercorarius longicaudus*	M	LC
Laridae (Gulls & Terns)				
Brown Noddy		*Anous stolidus*	C	LC
Black Noddy		*Anous minutus*	N	LC
Grey Noddy		*Anous albivittus*	N	LC
White Noddy		*Gygis alba*	N	LC
Red-billed Gull	Tarāpunga	*Chroicocephalus novaehollandiae*	N	LC
Black-billed Gull	Tarāpuka	*Chroicocephalus bulleri*	E	NT
Laughing Gull		*Leucophaeus atricilla*	V	LC
Franklin's Gull		*Leucophaeus pipixcan*	V	LC
Southern Black-backed Gull	Karoro	*Larus dominicanus*	N	LC
Sooty Tern		*Onychoprion fuscatus*	N	LC
Grey-backed Tern		*Onychoprion lunatus*	V	LC
Bridled Tern		*Onychoprion anaethetus*	V	LC
Little Tern	Tara Teo	*Sternula albifrons*	M	LC
Fairy Tern	Tara Iti	*Sternula nereis*	N	VU
Gull-billed Tern		*Gelochelidon nilotica*	V	LC
Australian Tern		*Gelochelidon macrotarsa*	C	LC
Caspian Tern	Taranui	*Hydroprogne caspia*	N	LC
Black Tern		*Chlidonias niger*	V	LC
White-winged Black Tern		*Chlidonias leucopterus*	M	LC
Whiskered Tern		*Chlidonias hybridus*	V	LC
Black-fronted Tern	Tarapirohe	*Chlidonias albostriatus*	E	EN
White-fronted Tern	Tara	*Sterna striata*	N	NT
Black-naped Tern		*Sterna sumatrana*	V	LC
Antarctic Tern		*Sterna vittata*	N	LC
Arctic Tern		*Sterna paradisaea*	M	LC
Common Tern		*Sterna hirundo*	V	LC
Crested Tern		*Thalasseus bergii*	V	LC
Phaethontidae (Tropicbirds)				
Red-tailed Tropicbird	Amokura	*Phaethon rubricauda*	N	LC
White-tailed Tropicbird		*Phaethon lepturus*	V	LC
Spheniscidae (Penguins)				
Emperor Penguin		*Aptenodytes forsteri*	V	NT
King Penguin	Tokoraki	*Aptenodytes patagonicus*	V	LC
Adelie Penguin		*Pygoscelis adeliae*	V	LC
Gentoo Penguin		*Pygoscelis papua*	V	LC
Chinstrap Penguin		*Pygoscelis antarcticus*	V	LC
Western Rockhopper Penguin		*Eudyptes chrysocome*	V	VU
Eastern Rockhopper Penguin	Tawaki Piki Toka	*Eudyptes filholi*	N	VU
Northern Rockhopper Penguin		*Eudyptes moseleyi*	V	EN
Fiordland Crested Penguin	Tawaki	*Eudyptes pachyrhynchus*	E	NT
Snares Crested Penguin	Pokotiwha	*Eudyptes robustus*	E	VU
Erect-crested Penguin	Tawaki Nana Hī	*Eudyptes sclateri*	E	EN
Royal Penguin		*Eudyptes chrysolophus*	V	VU
Yellow-eyed Penguin	Hoiho	*Megadyptes antipodes*	E	EN

Common Name	Māori name	Scientific Name	Status	IUCN
Magellanic Penguin		*Spheniscus magellanicus*	V	LC
Little Penguin	Kororā	*Eudyptula minor*	N	LC
Diomedeidae (Albatrosses)				
Snowy Albatross	Toroa	*Diomedea exulans*	M	VU
Antipodean Albatross	Toroa	*Diomedea antipodensis*	E	EN
Southern Royal Albatross	Toroa	*Diomedea epomophora*	E	VU
Northern Royal Albatross	Toroa	*Diomedea sanfordi*	E	EN
Black-footed Albatross		*Phoebastria nigripes*	V	NT
Laysan Albatross		*Phoebastria immutabilis*	V	NT
Atlantic Yellow-nosed Albatross		*Thalassarche chlororhynchos*	V	EN
Indian Yellow-nosed Albatross		*Thalassarche carteri*	C	EN
Grey-headed Albatross	Toroa	*Thalassarche chrysostoma*	N	EN
Black-browed Albatross	Toroa	*Thalassarche melanophris*	C	LC
Campbell Island Albatross	Toroa	*Thalassarche impavida*	E	VU
Buller's Albatross	Toroa	*Thalassarche bulleri*	E	NT
White-capped Albatross	Toroa	*Thalassarche cauta*	N	NT
Chatham Island Albatross	Toroa	*Thalassarche eremita*	E	VU
Salvin's Albatross	Toroa	*Thalassarche salvini*	N	VU
Sooty Albatross		*Phoebetria fusca*	V	EN
Light-mantled Sooty Albatross	Toroa Pango	*Phoebetria palpebrata*	N	NT
Oceanitidae (Austral Storm Petrels)				
Wilson's Storm Petrel		*Oceanites oceanicus*	M	LC
Grey-backed Storm Petrel	Reoreo	*Garrodia nereis*	N	LC
White-faced Storm Petrel	Takahikare	*Pelagodroma marina*	N	LC
Kermadec Storm Petrel		*Pelagodroma albiclunis*	E	CR
White-bellied Storm Petrel		*Fregetta grallaria*	N	LC
Black-bellied Storm Petrel	Takahikare-rangi	*Fregetta tropica*	N	LC
New Zealand Storm Petrel	Takahikare-raro	*Fregetta maoriana*	E	CR
Hydrobatidae (Northern Storm Petrels)				
Matsudaira's Storm Petrel		*Hydrobates matsudairae*	V	VU
Leach's Storm Petrel		*Hydrobates leucorhous*	V	VU
Procellariidae (Petrels, Shearwaters & Diving Petrels)				
Southern Giant Petrel	Pāngurunguru	*Macronectes giganteus*	M	LC
Northern Giant Petrel	Pāngurunguru	*Macronectes halli*	N	LC
Northern Fulmar		*Fulmarus glacialis*	V	LC
Antarctic Fulmar		*Fulmarus glacialoides*	M	LC
Antarctic Petrel		*Thalassoica antarctica*	V	LC
Cape Petrel	Karetai Hurukoko	*Daption capense*	N	LC
Kerguelen Petrel		*Lugensa brevirostris*	M	LC
Grey-faced Petrel	Ōi	*Pterodroma gouldi*	E	LC
White-headed Petrel		*Pterodroma lessonii*	N	LC
Providence Petrel		*Pterodroma solandri*	V	LC
Chatham Island Taiko	Tāiko	*Pterodroma magentae*	E	CR
Kermadec Petrel	Pia Koia	*Pterodroma neglecta*	N	LC
Herald Petrel		*Pterodroma heraldica*	V	LC
Phoenix Petrel		*Pterodroma alba*	V	VU
Soft-plumaged Petrel		*Pterodroma mollis*	N	LC
Mottled Petrel	Kōrure	*Pterodroma inexpectata*	E	NT
Juan Fernandez Petrel		*Pterodroma externa*	V	VU

Common Name	Māori name	Scientific Name	Status	IUCN
White-necked Petrel		*Pterodroma cervicalis*	N	VU
Black-winged Petrel	Karetai Kapa Mangu	*Pterodroma nigripennis*	N	LC
Chatham Petrel	Ranguru	*Pterodroma axillaris*	E	VU
Cook's Petrel	Tītī	*Pterodroma cookii*	E	VU
Stejneger's Petrel		*Pterodroma longirostris*	V	VU
Pycroft's Petrel		*Pterodroma pycrofti*	E	VU
Gould's Petrel		*Pterodroma leucoptera*	M	VU
Collared Petrel		*Pterodroma brevipes*	V	VU
Blue Petrel		*Halobaena caerulea*	M	LC
Broad-billed Prion	Pararā	*Pachyptila vittata*	N	LC
Salvin's Prion		*Pachyptila salvini*	M	LC
Antarctic Prion	Totorore	*Pachyptila desolata*	N	LC
Thin-billed Prion	Korotangi	*Pachyptila belcheri*	M	LC
Fairy Prion	Tītī wainui	*Pachyptila turtur*	N	LC
Pyramid Prion		*Pachyptila pyramidalis*	E	NT
Fulmar Prion		*Pachyptila crassirostris*	E	NT
Bulwer's Petrel		*Bulweria bulwerii*	V	LC
White-chinned Petrel	Karetai Kauae Mā	*Procellaria aequinoctialis*	N	VU
Westland Petrel	Tāiko	*Procellaria westlandica*	E	EN
Black Petrel	Tāiko	*Procellaria parkinsoni*	E	VU
Grey Petrel	Kuia	*Procellaria cinerea*	N	NT
Tahiti Petrel		*Pseudobulweria rostrata*	V	NT
Cory's Shearwater		*Calonectris borealis*	V	LC
Streaked Shearwater		*Calonectris leucomelas*	V	NT
Wedge-tailed Shearwater		*Ardenna pacifica*	N	LC
Buller's Shearwater	Rako	*Ardenna bulleri*	E	VU
Short-tailed Shearwater		*Ardenna tenuirostris*	M	LC
Sooty Shearwater	Tītī	*Ardenna grisea*	N	NT
Great Shearwater		*Ardenna gravis*	V	LC
Pink-footed Shearwater		*Ardenna creatopus*	V	VU
Flesh-footed Shearwater	Toanui	*Ardenna carneipes*	N	NT
Christmas Island Shearwater		*Puffinus nativitatis*	V	LC
Newell's Shearwater		*Puffinus auricularis*	V	CR
Manx Shearwater		*Puffinus puffinus*	V	LC
Fluttering Shearwater	Pakahā	*Puffinus gavia*	E	LC
Hutton's Shearwater	Kaikōura Tītī	*Puffinus huttoni*	E	EN
Little Shearwater	Totorore	*Puffinus assimilis*	N	LC
Subantarctic Shearwater		*Puffinus elegans*	N	LC
Common Diving Petrel	Kuaka	*Pelecanoides urinatrix*	N	LC
Whenua Hou Diving Petrel	Kuaka Whenua Hou	*Pelecanoides georgicus*	N	LC
Fregatidae (Frigatebirds)				
Great Frigatebird		*Fregata minor*	V	LC
Lesser Frigatebird		*Fregata ariel*	V	LC
Sulidae (Gannets & Boobies)				
Cape Gannet		*Morus capensis*	V	LC
Australasian Gannet	Tākapu	*Morus serrator*	N	LC
Red-footed Booby		*Sula sula*	V	LC
Brown Booby		*Sula leucogaster*	V	LC
Masked Booby		*Sula dactylatra*	N	LC
Anhingidae (Darters)				
Australasian Darter		*Anhinga novaehollandiae*	V	LC

Common Name	Māori name	Scientific Name	Status	IUCN
Phalacrocoracidae (Cormorants & Shags)				
Little Shag	Kawaupaka	Microcarbo melanoleucos	N	LC
Black Shag	Māpunga	Phalacrocorax carbo	N	LC
Pied Shag	Kāruhiruhi	Phalacrocorax varius	N	LC
Little Black Shag	Kawau Tūī	Phalacrocorax sulcirostris	N	LC
Spotted Shag	Kawau Tikitiki	Phalacrocorax punctatus	E	LC
Pitt Island Shag	Kawau o Rangihaute	Phalacrocorax featherstoni	E	EN
New Zealand King Shag	Kawau Pāteketeke	Leucocarbo carunculatus	E	VU
Otago Shag	Matapo	Leucocarbo chalconotus	E	VU
Foveaux Shag	Mapo	Leucocarbo stewarti	E	VU
Chatham Island Shag	Papua	Leucocarbo onslowi	E	VU
Bounty Island Shag		Leucocarbo ranfurlyi	E	VU
Auckland Island Shag	Kawau o Motu Maha	Leucocarbo colensoi	E	VU
Campbell Island Shag		Leucocarbo campbelli	E	VU
Macquarie Island Shag		Leucocarbo purpurascens	V	VU
Pelecanidae (Pelicans)				
Australian Pelican	Perikana	Pelecanus conspicillatus	V	LC
Ardeidae (Herons & Bitterns)				
Cattle Egret		Bubulcus ibis	M	LC
Grey Heron		Ardea cinerea	V	LC
Pacific Heron		Ardea pacifica	V	LC
White Heron	Kōtuku	Ardea alba	N	LC
Plumed Egret		Ardea intermedia	V	LC
White-faced Heron	Matuku Moana	Egretta novaehollandiae	N	LC
Little Egret		Egretta garzetta	V	LC
Reef Heron	Matuku Moana	Egretta sacra	N	LC
Nankeen Night Heron	Umu Kōtuku	Nycticorax caledonicus	C	LC
Australasian Bittern	Matuku-hūrepo	Botaurus poiciloptilus	N	EN
Australian Little Bittern		Ixobrychus dubius	V	LC
New Zealand Little Bittern	Kaoriki	Ixobrychus novaezelandiae	E	EX
Threskiornithidae (Ibises & Spoonbills)				
Glossy Ibis		Plegadis falcinellus	C	LC
White Ibis		Threskiornis molucca	V	LC
Straw-necked Ibis		Threskiornis spinicollis	V	LC
Royal Spoonbill	Kōtuku Ngutupapa	Platalea regia	N	LC
Yellow-billed Spoonbill		Platalea flavipes	V	LC
Accipitridae (Kites, Hawks & Eagles)				
Black Kite		Milvus migrans	V	LC
Swamp Harrier	Kāhu	Circus approximans	N	LC
White-bellied Sea Eagle		Haliaeetus leucogaster	V	LC
Tytonidae (Barn Owls)				
Barn Owl		Tyto alba	C	LC
Strigidae (Owls)				
Morepork	Ruru	Ninox novaeseelandiae	N	LC
Laughing Owl	Whēkau	Ninox albifacies	E	EX
Little Owl	Ruru Nohinohi	Athene noctua	I	LC
Coraciidae (Rollers)				
Dollarbird		Eurystomus orientalis	V	LC
Alcedinidae (Kingfishers)				
Laughing Kookaburra		Dacelo novaeguineae	I	LC
Sacred Kingfisher	Kōtare	Todiramphus sanctus	N	LC

Common Name	Māori name	Scientific Name	Status	IUCN
Falconidae (Falcons)				
Nankeen Kestrel		*Falco cenchroides*	V	LC
New Zealand Falcon	Kārearea	*Falco novaeseelandiae*	E	LC
Strigopidae (New Zealand Parrots)				
Kakapo	Kākāpō	*Strigops habroptila*	E	CR
Kaka	Kākā	*Nestor meridionalis*	E	EN
Kea	Kea	*Nestor notabilis*	E	EN
Cacatuidae (Cockatoos)				
Sulphur-crested Cockatoo		*Cacatua galerita*	I	LC
Galah		*Eolophus roseicapilla*	I	LC
Psittaculidae (Old World Parrots)				
Eastern Rosella	Kākā Uhi Whero	*Platycercus eximius*	I	LC
Red-crowned Parakeet	Kākāriki	*Cyanoramphus novaezelandiae*	N	LC
Yellow-crowned Parakeet	Kākāriki	*Cyanoramphus auriceps*	E	NT
Orange-fronted Parakeet	Kākāriki Karaka	*Cyanoramphus malherbi*	E	CR
Forbes' Parakeet		*Cyanoramphus forbesi*	E	VU
Antipodes Island Parakeet		*Cyanoramphus unicolor*	E	VU
Reischek's Parakeet		*Cyanoramphus hochstetteri*	E	VU
Acanthisittidae (New Zealand Wrens)				
Rifleman	Tītitipounamu	*Acanthisitta chloris*	E	LC
Bush Wren	Mātuhituhi	*Xenicus longipes*	E	EX
Rock Wren	Pīwauwau	*Xenicus gilviventris*	E	EN
Lyall's Wren		*Traversia lyalli*	E	EX
Meliphagidae (Honeyeaters)				
Bellbird	Korimako	*Anthornis melanura*	E	LC
Chatham Island Bellbird		*Anthornis melanocephala*	E	EX
Tui	Tūī	*Prosthemadera novaeseelandiae*	E	LC
Red Wattlebird		*Anthochaera carunculata*	V	LC
Acanthizidae (Australasian Warblers)				
Grey Warbler	Riroriro	*Gerygone igata*	E	LC
Chatham Island Warbler		*Gerygone albofrontata*	E	LC
Callaeidae (New Zealand Wattlebirds)				
North Island Kokako	Kōkako	*Callaeas wilsoni*	E	NT
South Island Kokako	Kōkā	*Callaeas cinereus*	E	CR/EX
North Island Saddleback	Tīeke	*Philesturnus rufusater*	E	NT
South Island Saddleback	Tīeke	*Philesturnus carunculatus*	E	NT
Huia	Huia	*Heteralocha acutirostris*	E	EX
Notiomystidae (Stitchbird)				
Stitchbird	Hihi	*Notiomystis cincta*	E	VU
Mohouidae (New Zealand Creepers)				
Whitehead	Pōpokotea	*Mohoua albicilla*	E	LC
Yellowhead	Mohua	*Mohoua ochrocephala*	E	EN
Brown Creeper	Pīpipi	*Mohoua novaeseelandiae*	E	LC
Oriolidae (Piopio)				
North Island Piopio	Piopio	*Turnagra tanagra*	E	EX
South Island Piopio	Piopio	*Turnagra capensis*	E	EX
Campephagidae (Cuckooshrikes)				
Black-faced Cuckoo-shrike		*Coracina novaehollandiae*	V	LC
White-winged Triller		*Lalage tricolor*	V	LC
Artamidae (Woodswallows & Butcherbirds)				
Masked Woodswallow		*Artamus personatus*	V	LC

Common Name	Māori name	Scientific Name	Status	IUCN
White-browed Woodswallow		*Artamus superciliosus*	V	LC
Dusky Woodswallow		*Artamus cyanopterus*	V	LC
Australian Magpie	Makipai	*Gymnorhina tibicen*	I	LC
Rhipiduridae (Fantails)				
New Zealand Fantail	Pīwakawaka	*Rhipidura fuliginosa*	N	LC
Willie Wagtail		*Rhipidura leucophrys*	V	LC
Monarchidae (Monarchs)				
Satin Flycatcher		*Myiagra cyanoleuca*	V	LC
Black-faced Monarch		*Monarcha melanopsis*	V	LC
Magpie-lark		*Grallina cyanoleuca*	V	LC
Corvidae (Crows)				
Rook		*Corvus frugilegus*	I	LC
Petroicidae (Australasian Robins)				
Tomtit	Miromiro	*Petroica macrocephala*	E	LC
Black Robin	Karure	*Petroica traversi*	E	VU
North Island Robin	Toutouwai	*Petroica longipes*	E	LC
South Island Robin	Kakaruai	*Petroica australis*	E	LC
Alaudidae (Larks)				
Eurasian Skylark	Kairaka	*Alauda arvensis*	I	LC
Acrocephalidae (Reed-warblers)				
Australian Reed-warbler		*Acrocephalus australis*	V	LC
Locustellidae (Grassbirds)				
Fernbird	Mātātā	*Poodytes punctatus*	E	LC
Chatham Island Fernbird		*Poodytes rufescens*	E	EX
Hirundinidae (Swallows & Martins)				
Welcome Swallow		*Hirundo neoxena*	N	LC
Fairy Martin		*Petrochelidon ariel*	V	LC
Tree Martin		*Petrochelidon nigricans*	V	LC
Zosteropidae (White-eyes)				
Silvereye		*Zosterops lateralis*	N	LC
Sturnidae (Starlings & Mynas)				
Common Starling	Tāringi	*Sturnus vulgaris*	I	LC
Common Myna	Maina	*Acridotheres tristis*	I	LC
Turdidae (Thrushes)				
Eurasian Blackbird	Manu Pango	*Turdus merula*	I	LC
Song Thrush	Manu-kai-hua-rakau	*Turdus philomelos*	I	LC
Prunellidae (Accentors)				
Dunnock		*Prunella modularis*	I	LC
Passeridae (Old World Sparrows)				
House Sparrow	Tiu	*Passer domesticus*	I	LC
Motacillidae (Pipits)				
New Zealand Pipit	Pīhoihoi	*Anthus novaeseelandiae*	E	LC
Fringillidae (Finches)				
Eurasian Chaffinch	Pahirini	*Fringilla coelebs*	I	LC
European Greenfinch		*Chloris chloris*	I	LC
Redpoll		*Acanthis flammea*	I	LC
European Goldfinch	Kōurarini	*Carduelis carduelis*	I	LC
Emberizidae (Buntings)				
Yellowhammer	Hurukōwhai	*Emberiza citrinella*	I	LC
Cirl Bunting		*Emberiza cirlus*	I	LC

birdsnz.org.nz Birds New Zealand (The Ornithological Society for New Zealand) offers monthly meetings across the country in addition to a nationwide annual conference for people to share in the study, knowledge and enjoyment of birds.

birdingnz.net/forum/ Online forum for the discussion of all things to do with wild birds in New Zealand, including birding spots and trip reports, rare bird sightings, organized events and more.

nzbirdsonline.org.nz Easy-to-use encyclopaedia of all the bird species found in New Zealand, with comprehensive information compiled from verified sources and extensive catalogue of photographs.

merlin.allaboutbirds.org Free app to help familiarise yourself with the birds of a particular region, with photos, facts, and calls from the eBird archives.

xeno-canto.org Free online database of bird calls from around the world.

doc.govt.nz The Department of Conservation is the government branch tasked with conserving New Zealand's natural and historic heritage, as well as educating the public on the benefits of doing so. There is an extensive range of volunteering options available, some of which are the only way to visit protected island sanctuaries and experience the most precious species, such as the Black Robin and Kākāpō.

forestandbird.org.nz New Zealand's leading independent conservation organization, with more than 80,000 members. Many opportunities are presented, from engaging with the public sector on conservation issues, to helping out with local restoration projects. Members receive a quarterly magazine. The youth chapter Kiwi Conservation Club (KCC) helps bring those aged 5–13 closer to nature. For those aged 14–25 it also offers Forest & Bird Youth, run by young people for young people who want to harness their passion to create change in New Zealand today.

birdrescue.org.nz Information on how to handle an injured or abandoned bird, as well as where to find your local rescue centre. Note that if you find a chick, sometimes the best thing to do is to leave it where you found it or in a safe space nearby.

This book is dedicated to the wonderful Liz Light, who I was lucky to collaborate with on *The 50 Best Birdwatching Sites in NZ* after she asked to include some of my photographs. Liz had such a unique and thoughtful way of describing the nature surrounding her, as it did at all times. Liz kindly got me the offer for this publication, and for that I will be always grateful to her. She was encouraging and helpful until the very end.

To John Beaufoy and Rosemary Wilkinson for entrusting me, both fresh out of high school and in the middle of an international youth exchange to Belgium, with the task of creating this book on the very topic I am most passionate about. And to Krystyna Mayer for her meticulous editing – it has been a pleasure to work together.

À ma famille d'accueil, Christine et Stéphane qui m'ont soutenus au début de ce livre pendant mon échange en Belgique. And to my parents Lucy and Peter who supported me from afar and on my return home to New Zealand.

To Imogen Warren, Charlie Barnett, and Matthias Dehling, Scott Brooks, David Boyle, and Bradley Shields, an immense thank you for your generous photographic contributions that elevate this book to a whole new level. And thanks to Leon Berard, Adam Colley, George Hobson, Darren Markin, Colin O'Donnell, Max de Beer, Allan MacGillivray, Aaron Skelton, Giverny Kate Forbes, Phil Battley, David Thomas and Nick Beckwith, for being extremely helpful in sourcing and providing additional photos. Without all of you, this would not have been possible.

Finally, thank you to all those who have put up with me over the last 10 years, driven me to amazing new places, and helped my passion to grow and flourish. Thank you to my much-loving family, my fellow young birders, all the kind-hearted people of Birds Auckland and Tiritiri Matangi Supporters, my supportive friends at Otago University, on exchange and beyond, and of course my primary school teacher Sonya Galbraith – your passion was the spark for all this.

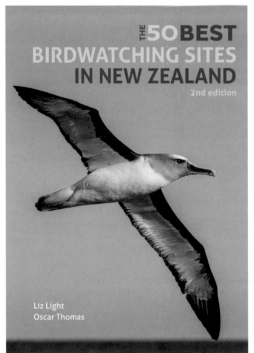

▪ INDEX ▪

■ INDEX ■